HOW TO START

In this Series

How to Apply for a Job
How to Apply to an Industrial Tribunal
How to Be a Freelance Secretary
How to Be a Freelance Journalist
How to Be a Local Councillor
How to Be an Effective School Governor
How to Become an Au Pair
How to Buy & Run a Shop
How to Buy & Run a Small Hotel
How to Choose a Private School
How to Claim State Benefits
How to Communicate at Work
How to Conduct Staff Appraisals
How to Counsel People at Work
How to Do Voluntary Work Abroad
How to Do Your Own Advertising
How to Do Your Own PR
How to Emigrate
How to Employ & Manage Staff
How to Enjoy Retirement
How to Find Temporary Work Abroad
How to Get a Job Abroad
How to Get a Job in America
How to Get a Job in Australia
How to Get a Job in Europe
How to Get a Job in France
How to Get a Job in Germany
How to Get a Job in Hotels & Catering
How to Get a Job in Travel & Tourism
How to Get Into Films & TV
How to Get Into Radio
How to Get That Job
How to Help Your Child at School
How to Invest in Stocks & Shares
How to Keep Business Accounts
How to Know Your Rights at Work
How to Know Your Rights: Students
How to Know Your Rights: Teachers
How to Live & Work in America
How to Live & Work in Australia
How to Live & Work in Belgium
How to Live & Work in France
How to Live & Work in Germany
How to Live & Work in the Gulf
How to Live & Work in Hong Kong
How to Live & Work in Italy
How to Live & Work in Japan
How to Live & Work in New Zealand
How to Live & Work in Portugal
How to Live & Work in Saudi Arabia
How to Live & Work in Spain
How to Lose Weight & Keep Fit
How to Make a Wedding Speech
How to Manage a Sales Team
How to Manage Budgets & Cash Flows
How to Manage Computers at Work
How to Manage People at Work
How to Manage Your Career
How to Master Book-Keeping
How to Master Business English
How to Master GCSE Accounts
How to Master Languages
How to Master Public Speaking
How to Pass Exams Without Anxiety
How to Pass That Interview
How to Plan a Wedding
How to Prepare Your Child for School
How to Publish a Book
How to Publish a Newsletter
How to Raise Business Finance
How to Raise Funds & Sponsorship
How to Rent & Buy Property in France
How to Rent & Buy Property in Italy
How to Retire Abroad
How to Return to Work
How to Run a Local Campaign
How to Run a Voluntary Group
How to Sell Your Business
How to Spend a Year Abroad
How to Start a Business from Home
How to Start a New Career
How to Start Word Processing
How to Start Your Own Business
How to Study Abroad
How to Study & Learn
How to Study & Live in Britain
How to Survive at College
How to Survive Divorce
How to Take Care of Your Heart
How to Teach Abroad
How to Travel Round the World
How to Understand Finance at Work
How to Use a Library
How to Work from Home
How to Work in an Office
How to Work with Dogs
How to Write a Press Release
How to Write a Report
How to Write an Assignment
How to Write an Essay
How to Write Business Letters
How to Write for Publication
How to Write for Television

Other titles in preparation

START WORD PROCESSING

A step-by-step guide for beginners

Ian Phillipson

How To Books

By the same author
How to Do Your Own PR
How to Work from Home

British Library Cataloguing in Publication Data
A catalogue record for this book is available from the British Library.

First published in 1995 by How To Books Ltd, Plymbridge House, Estover Road, Plymouth PL6 7PZ, United Kingdom. Tel: Plymouth (01752) 735251/ 695745. Fax: (01752) 695699. Telex: 45635.

Note: The material contained in this book is set out in good faith for general guidance and no liability can be accepted for loss or expense incurred as a result of relying in particular circumstances on statements made in the book. The law and regulations are complex and liable to change, and readers should check the current position with the relevant authorities before making personal arrangements.

Typeset by Concept Communications (Design & Print) Ltd, Crayford, Kent.
Printed and bound by The Cromwell Press, Broughton Gifford, Melksham, Wiltshire.

Contents

List of Illustrations

Preface

For thousands of years humans have used writing as a permanent form of conveying their thoughts, ideas and messages. But from the outset, when sticks were used to write in clay or on stone through to even the electric typewriter, writing suffered from one basic problem: once something was written down, the words used to write it could not be used again — they were wasted and gone.

But with the arrival of the microchip, which can store information electronically, that all changed. Now anyone who wrote could re-use the words they had written.

Thanks to that electronic revolution we now have word processing, a wonderful way to write because it lets you change, move and present your words in the way that suits you best. In the modern world an ability to word process is a valuable skill, opening up career opportunities, allowing you to do your job more effectively and to complete written work from college assignments to books, quicker and better.

Even if you know little or nothing about modern technology this book will help you, because it deals in basic principles. This makes it the ideal starting point if you want to know more about the subject before committing yourself to a particular type of word processor, investing in equipment or even enrolling on a word processing course.

However, given that there are so many word processors on the market today, each with their own particular way of working, there is just not the space to make this a totally comprehensive guide to word processing. Therefore this book lets you dip a foot in the water. To learn more about word processing you will simply have to sit down at the keyboard with your own word processor's manual and begin to work through it. The more time that you can spend practising word processing skills the better you will become. And rather like learning a language, when you have mastered one particular word processor you will find it much easier to understand another one. Indeed, making an extra effort to learn several can be extremely valuable in the work place because it makes you a far more flexible commodity.

The keys to word processing success are literally in your own hands.

Ian Phillipson

1
Do You Need Word Processing?

HOW WORD PROCESSING HELPS

Most of us write something every day. It might be just a note or a letter, or something longer, perhaps a report or even a book. A pen or even a pencil may be fine for this if you are writing a letter or note to a friend or a relative, but if you want to influence or to impress someone with your words, this is no good at all.

Until a few years ago, the only way to produce a more businesslike document was by using a typewriter. But this has two major disadvantages.

Firstly, unless you're a good typist, typewriting isn't a quick means of writing because your finger movements are hesitant and inefficient. What's more, if you aren't a good typist you also tend to make a lot of mistakes. Correcting these not only slows you down further, but also means your final piece of work can look badly presented.

Secondly, once you've typed out your words you can't use them again. That's it. They are dead and gone. Even if you keep a carbon copy of the letter or document, you can't send it to someone else. You can only use it for reference.

However, the last 20 years have seen a writing revolution thanks to the computer.

Computers used to be very large and highly expensive machines that could be afforded only by the largest of companies and operated only by highly trained personnel. Now computers have become everyday objects found in homes and offices up and down the country.

Not only are computers very good at performing monotonous and routine tasks, but they can also tackle a very wide range of more complicated jobs, including those done by the typewriter. And when a computer takes on the role of a typewriter then it's not called typing any more but **word processing**, and that is the subject of this book.

Word processing isn't a difficult subject to understand or to learn. It

IS THIS YOU?

Writer
Journalist
Teacher
Librarian
Researcher
Business person
Clerk
Telephonist
Student
College leaver
Temporary assistant
Charity worker
Church worker
Franchisee
Curator
Event organiser
Office worker
Artist
Designer
Photographer
Sales person
PR consultant
Accountant
Receptionist
Publisher
Mail order agent
Trainer
Club secretary
Manager
Would-be entrepreneur
Accountant
Local councillor
Committee member
Action group member
Fundraiser
Market researcher
Solicitor
Trade union official
Management consultant
Estate agent
Travel agent
Hotelier
Advisor
Counsellor
Credit control clerk
Filing clerk
Marketing assistant
Office junior
Secretarial assistant
Accounts clerk
Production assistant
Archives assistant
Customer services assistant
Order clerk
Officer supervisor
Personal assistant
Financial consultant
Publican
Jobseeker
Book keeper
College staff
Garden centre owner
Local authority manager
Storekeeper
Tourist attraction owner
Theatre manager
Interior designer

is simply a term for the typing and editing of words and documents (letters, memos, articles, reports and books) on a computer screen. It can be as simple or as complicated as you wish to make it.

In order to take the mystery out of word processing *How to Start Word Processing* will concentrate on basic principles, rather than on the specifics of any one particular word processing product, which all have their own specific way of working.

To learn more about particular word processors you should consult their manuals or user guides.

SAVING YOU TIME

When you use a normal typewriter, to obtain more than one copy you have to type your document out all over again, or make a photocopy or use carbon paper. This is not a problem when using a word processor.

If you want to write the exact same letter twice, you only need to type it once. The word processor will remember what you have typed and then produce a second copy for you, as and when you want it. And if you want to type a letter that's only slightly different then all you need to do is make changes to the original.

What's more, your word processor will remember your words for as long as you want it to, whether that's a matter of minutes, days, months or even years. All you have to do is ask the word processor to retrieve the words and off you go again.

CUTTING DOWN ON ERRORS

Normally with a typewriter when you hit one of its keys you immediately type a character onto a sheet of paper. This is fine if you are an accurate typist, but what if you aren't and you make a mistake? Then you either have to hide your error with correction fluid and type over it, or you have to pull out that first sheet of paper, put a new one into the machine and start all over again.

You don't have that problem with a word processor because it doesn't immediately put characters down on to a sheet of paper. So, if you make a mistake you can change what you have written before it's committed to paper. You can do this because your word processor remembers your words before typing them out and only prints them on to paper when you tell it to. So you don't have to be a very good, accurate or fast typist to use a word processor. In fact a word processor can make anyone a reasonable typist.

MAKING ROUTINE CHORES EASY

Another advantage of a word processor is that you can ask it to do routine tasks automatically so you don't have to be bothered with them. For instance, if you had just finished writing a book and then suddenly decided to change the name of your main character, there's no problem. You simply ask the word processor to do it for you. You can also ask the word processor to insert blocks of text that you use frequently, such as your name and address, without typing them out each time.

MAKING YOUR WORK LOOK BETTER

There really is only so much you can do with a typewriter. It does let you put your words in a particular place on the page, if you are skillful enough, but that's about it. A word processor does far more. Not only will it allow you to alter the size, shape and position of words and letters, but it will also allow you to incorporate graphics and pictures into your document to make it look eye-catching and different. You can also use other products on your computer to combine information from several sources so as to create a highly useful document or report.

WORKING WITH OTHERS

One of the distinctive features of computers and word processing is that it is possible to do work on one word processor and then take it to another. This means that you can complete previously started work elsewhere, or even hand the document over to someone else to finish.

INCREASING YOUR PRODUCTIVITY

By now you should have a good idea of how much writing flexibility and power a word processor gives you in comparison with a standard, and now rather old-fashioned, typewriter. Even with the little knowledge you have so far of word processing you should be able to see ways in which it can save you time and effort when writing anything. And this is only just the tip of the word processing iceberg: there is much, much more to come.

THE DISADVANTAGES OF WORD PROCESSING

Firstly, you will probably have to spend a little more on equipment than you would with a typewriter, but the investment is worth it.

Secondly, if you aren't used to working with computers or other types of modern technology then you might find working with a word processor a little daunting at first.

Thirdly, though word processing is a relatively easy skill to learn, it still will take a little longer to learn than conventional typing.

Fourthly, some people who write fiction and other forms of creative writing find it hinders their thought processes and creativity. However, most people don't see this as a problem.

WHO CAN BENEFIT FROM WORD PROCESSING?

Keyboard skills and a knowledge of what computers can do (particularly such a versatile skill as word processing), are becoming increasingly important and often fundamental to many jobs and activities in the modern world.

Indeed, literally any office job will require you to have some knowledge of word processing.

Word processing is for anyone who needs to write in their daily lives, whether for work or at home. Obviously it's a valuable skill for writers, authors and journalists, secretaries and personal assistants, but it can also be highly beneficial to officers of voluntary groups, church officials, organisers, women returners, students, business people, shopkeepers, executives and many, many others.

HOW COULD WORD PROCESSING HELP YOU?

Write down five areas in which you use words regularly in your everyday life:

1 . . . .

2 . . . .

3 . . . .

4 . . . .

5 . . . .

From what you've read so far, write down at least one advantage of word processing for each of these areas. The same advantage might crop up more than once.

1 . . . .

2 . . . .

3 . . . .

4 . . . .

5 . . . .

Do you need word processing?

Do you write many letters, memos or reports? Yes No

Do you write a number of similar letters that need just a slight alteration or change before they can be sent out? Yes No

Do you create documents that need to look good and impress others? Yes No

Are you a poor typist? Yes No

Do you need to produce written work quickly? Yes No

Do you need to combine words with tables and other illustrations in a single document? Yes No

Do you need regularly to update the information in reports, standard letters, price lists and other such documents? Yes No

Do you need to produce written work jointly with others? Yes No

A number of Yes answers suggests that word processing is definitely for you.

CASE STUDIES

Throughout this book we will dip into the experiences of four very different people who all decide that word processing will help them in their daily lives.

Jane, the student

It's Jane's first year at college. The essays are coming at her thick and fast, so that she seems to spend nearly all her time scribbling furiously on A4 sheets, wearing out pens and watching her handwriting get worse and worse as she writes faster and faster. Already she has been warned by her tutor that he's having difficulty reading some of her work. He has even marked her down for it. The situation is made even worse by the fact that a growing number of the other students on her course are using computers and word processors to produce good looking work, which even the tutor with the poorest eyesight in the world can easily read.

Jane knows that it's only human nature for her tutor to compare the immaculately typed work with her own for her to come out worse. She decides that she's not going to let that happen and decides to buy her own computer. She begins to count the pennies remaining in her grant and asks a few 'technical' friends about buying computers.

Alex, the accountant

Alex runs a one-man accountancy practice. He already uses a computer to a certain extent for doing his clients' accounts. The typing of letters he leaves to a part-time secretary who comes in for a couple of mornings each week to use the electric typewriter. If Alex has an urgent letter that he wants to get out, he'll attempt to type it himself. But 90 per cent of the time he wastes an hour or more trying to produce something that's good enough to send to a client. In the end he generally gives up in frustration and waits until the secretary arrives the next day or the day after. When one client berates him for his slowness in not getting out a letter sooner, Alex knows that he has to invest in word processing.

Pam, the secretary

As secretary to the managing director of a large engineering company, Pam had among her many talents very good keyboard skills. But that was 15 years ago. Since then she has brought up a family, who are now old enough to fend for themselves. So, Pam is thinking about taking up some part-time secretarial work. She applies for 12 jobs and manages to obtain a couple of interviews. However, not only is her interview technique quite rusty, but prospective employers constantly ask her what she knows about word processing. Each time she has to admit her ignorance.

It becomes increasingly obvious to Pam that though would-be employers are clearly interested in the quality of work she is capable of offering and in her background, they are put off by her lack of word processing knowledge. If she is going to get back into the job market, even for just a few hours a week, then she is going to have to close that rather large chink in her armour.

Michael, the author

With numerous articles, a radio play and a couple of books under his belt, Michael is a well-established writer who has been turning out words for the last ten years. Editors demand that he supplies his work neatly and carefully typed up. This he does using an electronic typewriter, but only after he has done all his preliminary thinking and rough drafts on the A4 blocks of paper he buys from Woolworth.

Michael has never worked in any other way, but it does mean that he spends a lot of time repeating his efforts, first writing out one draft, then a better draft, and then a third. For one radio play he wrote out five drafts in longhand before typing out the final script, which he had to do very carefully as he still is not a good typist. He sometimes feels frustrated at the length of time it takes him to complete his work and is looking to increase his output. He appreciates that word processing might help him produce more work, but is fearful that working in what he sees as a rather 'mechanical and electronic' fashion would cripple his creativity. In the end Michael's desire to produce more work overcomes his reservations and he decides to bite the word processing bullet.

2
Choosing the Equipment You Need

Just as with typing, word processing involves a keyboard, but that is largely where the similarities stop. Indeed, comparing a typewriter with a word processor is rather like comparing a Mini with a Ferrari. They both can take you places, but do so in very different ways and styles.

WHAT YOU NEED TO START

Word processing is done on a computer. This is made up of three parts:

- a **keyboard** on which you type
- a monitor screen or **visual display unit** (VDU), like a small television screen on which those words appear
- a **system unit** which is the box containing all the electronic and mechanical components of the computer.

In computing language this equipment is known as **hardware**.

A computer can't word process (or do any other sort of computing job) without the help of something called **software**. This is a set of electronic instructions that tells the computer how to do something. These instructions are stored on magnetic disks. There are two kinds of these: floppy and hard disks.

Floppy disks

Rather confusingly floppy disks aren't disk-shaped, but thin square-shaped packages either 3.5" or 5.25" in width. What is more, the smaller of the two aren't floppy at all, but come in rigid plastic cases that would break rather than flop. The larger floppies **are** bendable and have to be treated with more respect. They are also less commonly used than the smaller, rigid, disks.

To give the information that they hold to the computers, floppy disks have to be inserted into a slot in the computer. When the disk is in the slot it is sitting in a **disk drive** which makes the disk spin rapidly. When the disk is spinning it can pass on information to the computer or have data from the computer passed to it.

Hard disks

The second type of disk is known as the hard disk. This is hidden in the system unit box and remains there permanently. It works in a similar way to the floppy drive and disk, passing information to and from the rest of the computer. However, in several ways it is crucially different:

- A hard disk holds far more information than a floppy disk. If you think of the floppy disk as being like a paperback novel and the hard disk as being like the *Encyclopedia Britannica* (or even several copies of it) you will have some idea of the difference. The information can include not just the software that tells your computer what to do, but also all the documents you are working on currently and many others you have worked on over the months or years.

- The hard disk works faster than a floppy disk so you can write information on to it more quickly and retrieve information from it more quickly.

- You don't have to keep taking out and putting in new floppy disks if you want to recall other information or store extra data.

- Some software (including word processing programs) only works on computers with a suitably large hard drive.

- Work done on the word processor is far more difficult to find when everything is kept on floppy disks rather than all on a hard drive.

CHOOSING A COMPUTER

What type of computer?

Though there are many different makes of computer on sale, there are still only a few types to choose from.

The IBM compatible
The first and most common type is the IBM compatible Personal Computer, or PC. This type of machine is the one traditionally used for office and word processing work. Because there are many of them around they are relatively cheap and easy to buy. When you want this type of computer to do something you will generally have to type the instructions using the machine's keyboard. This is appreciated by people who are experienced typists.

The Apple Macintosh
The second type of computer you are likely to come across is made by Apple Macintosh. These machines are known as 'Apples', 'Macs', or 'Apple Macs'. They are more expensive than IBM PCs, but many people like them because they are easy to use. They are also particularly good if you want to produce not only words but also graphics and illustrations.

You tell Macs what to do by using not only a keyboard but also a device known as a **mouse**. This is a small plastic box which you push across a flat surface in order to move a pointer around the monitor screen to point at pictures or symbols, known as **icons**. These icons represent particular activities or functions that the software can do. Issuing commands in this way is easy, which makes using these machines enjoyable for those who don't like keyboards or who are not used to computers.

At one time there was a great deal of difference between these two types of computer but that is now changing with the introduction of new software (known as 'Windows') that makes the IBM type PCs easier and more like Apple Macs to use.

CHOOSING SPECIFIC FEATURES

Of the many tasks that a computer can perform, word processing is one of those that it finds easiest. For this reason you don't need the best or most expensive computer in the world. However, there are still certain features that you must watch out for so you don't end up with a machine that can't do what you want it to, or a very expensive machine that is too high powered and sophisticated for what you want to do.

Computer power
Just like cars, computers have different potential speeds and powers. This is determined by an electronic chip within them that is known as a **processor**. You will probably come across three different types of

processor: the 286, the 386 or the 486. The 286 processor is found in older machines, while the 486 is a more recent processor which makes the computer work a lot faster. Indeed, so crucial is the processor that computers are often classified by their processor: for instance you will hear people talk of 'a 386 or a 486'.

For word processing you do not need a fast computer (this book was written on a 286 machine), though if you intend to use the Windows-based software mentioned above then you will need at least a 386 machine. However, when buying any computer it is always sensible to think ahead. With modern technology moving forward so quickly you might find it sensible to buy a faster machine than you need right now to allow for any changes to your needs.

Hard disk size

It is always astute to buy a computer with as large a hard disk as you can afford. Not only will the hard disk fill up with your own documents faster than ever you imagined possible, but modern software can take up an awful lot of room in its own right. And if you want to do other things with your computer, such as create accounts, hold a database of information, or start desktop publishing, then disk space will be eaten up astonishingly quickly.

The size of the hard disk is measured in megabytes (Mb). To give you an idea of how much information can be held on a hard disk, a 40 Mb disk (which is small these days) can hold several books each of 100,000 words. For storing a moderate amount of information think in terms of 120 Mb hard disk.

Monitor screen

These can be black and white or colour and of various sizes. For word processing you will need something in the range of a 14 inch wide monitor, though a larger size will make it easier to see your work, especially if your eyesight is not all that it might be. A colour monitor isn't essential for word processing, but it does create a more pleasant and interesting tool to work with. It also allows you to mark blocks of text in colour, rather like being able to mark your document with colour felt tip pens or highlighters.

CHOOSING A PRINTER

It's all very well to create a document on your computer screen, but you will need a **printer** to put it onto paper. There are a number of types of printer you can choose from. Which is most suitable for you will depend on the speed at which you want to print, the quality of what you want to print and your budget.

- **Dot matrix printers** are at the cheap and cheerful end of the printer market. They work by pushing blunt pins against an ink ribbon which is then forced onto paper. By altering the formation of these pins, the printer can produce a wide range of letters, numbers, characters and shapes. These printers are noisy, quite slow and can't produce a very high quality of print, though many claim to achieve 'near letter quality' (NLQ) by printing over each character several times. If you look closely at the print from a dot matrix you can see that it is made up from a pattern of dots which can leave the edge of each letter looking slightly ragged and rough.

- **Daisywheel printers** produce better quality text than dot matrix printers because they work in a similar way to typewriters, pushing complete characters against an ink ribbon which then presses on to the paper. They are slower than dot matrix printers in operation and can't print a letter, character, number or typeface that isn't found on the 'print wheel' they are currently using. Therefore you can't produce a different typeface or size of type without changing the print wheel and you can't print graphics or illustrations at all. Daisywheel printers are also quite noisy. However, because they are rather old fashioned you can pick then up cheaply. Both the dot matrix and daisywheel printer have 'platens' around which the paper is rolled, just as typewriters do.

- **Ink jet and bubble-jet printers** fire a quick drying ink on to paper in the shape of the character you want. These are fast and can produce a wide number of different print styles, sizes of character and illustrations to a very high quality. Running costs can be high because the ink cartridges might need replacing frequently.

- **Laser printers** are at the very top end of the printer market and so are the most expensive. They work rather like a photocopier by firing a fine black dust on to the paper. They produce a very high quality image, which can be either text or illustration. If you have a good enough laser printer then you can use it to produce work of such good quality that it can be used as a master from which to produce brochures, letterheads or magazines. This can save you a lot of money if you frequently have to have material professionally printed. Laser printers are quiet.

The paper that ink-jet, bubble-jet and laser printers use is stored flat in a tray from where it is automatically fed to the printer.

WHERE TO BUY COMPUTER EQUIPMENT

- **High street stores** are convenient but offer a limited range and not a great deal of after sales service, if any.
- **Computer stores** offer good prices and a wide range, but may be some distance away from your home. They also might not provide much in the way of after sales support.
- **Computer dealers** are generally more expensive than the stores, but should give you the best after sales service and support. However, they can come across as being too technical and unapproachable for the novice computer user.
- **Mail order suppliers** advertise in national newspapers and computer magazines. They generally sell computer and word processing equipment at very good prices, but you should make sure that you are buying from a reputable supplier. Some of the computer magazines in which they run ads provide indemnity schemes. Buying from mail order suppliers is convenient, but you should find out as much as you can about particular machines by trying them out at stores first.
- **Auctions** can be good places to pick up computer equipment, often for a fifth of the retail price. That said, there are no guarantees as to the quality of the equipment and you are likely to have little if any comeback should anything go wrong. Go with an experienced computer user who can test the machines if you intend to buy this way.
- Buying **secondhand** can certainly deliver good bargains, just as with auctions, but again you have no guarantees that the equipment will work. If you do buy secondhand then try out the computer and software before handing over money. Again take an experienced computer user with you.

HOW TO LOOK AFTER YOUR EQUIPMENT

When you spend hard-earned cash on your computer equipment it is well worth taking pains to protect it by taking a few simple precautions.

- Cover the **keyboard** with a plastic sheet or specially designed cover at the end of every day. This stops dust getting into the works. Likewise cover the **screen** with cling film if there is a danger of coffee, tea or another liquid being splashed near or on your computer. For the keyboard you can buy proprietary covers.

- Use **cleaning fluids** that are designed for the computer when you clean it.

- Check the **wiring** of your computer monitor and printer every couple of weeks as screws can work loose.

- **Never** turn off your computer or word processor without going through the proper turning off procedure. Your computer manual will tell you what this is.

- Be extremely careful about putting **borrowed floppy disks** into your machine. These may contain rogue programs called viruses that can destroy information on your hard disk. You should check your computer frequently for viruses using anti-virus software.

Looking after your floppy disks

If you don't look after your floppy disks you can damage or even destroy the information stored on them. Therefore it makes sense to take care of floppy disks, particularly if you use them for storage of back up material.

- Take care when handling disks, even if some of them appear quite rigid in their stiff plastic casings. In particular do not touch any black magnetic surface that you might see (particularly easily done on 5.25" disks), or the exposed area in the middle of the disk. Fingerprints can easily damage the disk.

- Never bend the disk, or force it into a disk drive.

- Never put anything on top of a disk. The weight could cause damage.

- Keep drinks and foods away from them, as crumbs and liquids quickly cause problems. For the same reason you should avoid drinking and eating near your computer altogether.

- Keep your disks away from magnets. There are a lot of hidden magnets around, so be careful. You can find them in televisions and telephones.
- Don't use paperclips to attach bits of paper to a disk. Use sticky labels to write information on them. And when you use a label, write it before you stick it on the disk. Writing the label after you have stuck it on the disk can damage the disk no matter how gently you think you are writing.
- When a disk is not in use, keep it in a protective envelope or container, particularly if it is the more delicate 5.25" variety.
- Don't use disks that have become damaged or corrupted. They can damage your disk drive.
- When not in use, store your disks in a disk box. This will keep them out of harm's way and ensure that you always know where they are.

CHOOSING WORD PROCESSING SOFTWARE

There are literally hundreds of word processing packages around, ranging from simple ones that only do the basics to the very sophisticated and comprehensive, such as market leaders Ami Pro and WordPerfect. Which product you choose will depend on what you want your word processor to do and how much you want to spend.

Don't expect to find the perfect software. Even the most expensive, with all their extensive range of features, will have at least one shortcoming.

Telling the computer what to do

Mention has already been made of the differences between software programs, but now it's time to take a closer look at the ways in which they differ.

Though all word processing software does essentially the same thing, the main differences lie in the way in which you tell them to do something.

Using the keyboard

Until recently commands were given to nearly all computers by pressing sequences of keys on the keyboard. The main disadvantage of this is that sometimes these key sequences can be quite complicated and therefore difficult to remember, especially if you are using a top of the range word processor which has a lot of commands. If you can't remember the sequences then you can always write them down, but this is slow and distracting as you have to continually stop work and look up each command. What is more there is no consistency in these instructions and commands between different word processing packages, so you have to learn a new set of key commands when you start using a different word processor.

Despite these difficulties many word processors, including some of the leading ones, still use the keyboard as their main method of issuing commands.

Using menus

To overcome the problem of having to remember complicated key sequences some word processors let you call up lists of commands called menus onto the screen. A menu is merely a list of things that you can do. Fig. 1. shows a drop-down menu from the word processing package Wordperfect.

Retrieve	Shft-F10
Save	F10
Text In	Ctrl-F5
Text Out	Ctrl-F5
Password	Ctrl-F5
List Files	F5
Summary	
Print	Shft-F7
Setup	Shft-F1
Go to Dos	Ctrl-F5
Exit	F7

Fig. 1: A drop-down menu from the WordPerfect package.

You then choose which command you want to use by moving a highlighted bar up and down. Alternatively you can simply hit the key (highlighted) letter for each command: for example, the command Save would be activated by pressing S, and Retrieve by pressing R. Usually the highlighted letter will be the first letter of that command's name, but sometimes it is another letter if two commands in the same menu or Command Bar begin with the same letter.

Using a mouse

As word processors have become increasingly complicated by offering the user more and more commands that perhaps can only be issued by holding down three keys at one time, the mouse is increasingly being used by word processing packages as the simplest way of telling the computer what to do. It makes it easier for many people to operate a computer because they don't have to remember or issue commands through the keyboard but instead point at the pictures (icons) which represent the things they want their computer to do. For instance, if you wanted to dump some of your words you would just move your mouse pointer to the icon of a waste-paper basket. If you wanted to print your document then you would go to the icon of a printer perhaps.

When a mouse is plugged in to the computer an **arrow pointer** appears on the monitor screen and it is ready to use. Then all you have to do is place the mouse on a flat surface with your hand resting lightly on top. As you move the mouse around, the arrow pointer will mirror the movements of the mouse. When you have moved the pointer to the command icon or place where you want to be on screen, you can tell the computer to do something by clicking a button on top of the mouse. Using the mouse you can also move objects and text around on the monitor screen.

Windows-based software and Apple Macs use a mouse to issue commands. However, even if you use a mouse to issue commands you will still need the keyboard to type in text.

The advantages

- it is a very quick method of issuing commands
- it is a very easy way of issuing commands
- you don't have to remember lots of key combinations to issue commands

- many of the word processors that use a mouse to issue commands do so in a very similar way, so you don't have the trouble of having to learn a whole new range of command keys.

The disadvantages

- to use a mouse you have to take one hand off the keyboard a lot of the time; experienced touch typists think this slows them down
- if there is little room on your desk or if it regularly becomes cluttered you may not find it easy to make enough room to move a mouse around
- some people just don't like issuing commands in this highly visual way
- you may have to use it for issuing commands that you feel more at home with issuing through the keyboard
- to use a mouse you have to master 'double clicking': ie clicking a button on top of the mouse twice, very quickly.

CHECKLIST

1. Besides writing, do you also want to use your computer for doing accounts, or storing lots of files on customers, suppliers etc? Yes No

If Yes, then you need a faster computer than if you were just going to do word processing. Unfortunately, the faster the computer, the more expensive it is to buy. It is very useful to have a fast computer if you need to manipulate a lot of data or accounts.

2. Do you need to save a lot of information? Yes No

It's still possible to buy a computer that doesn't have a hard disk, but why would you want to? See above for all the reasons why a computer without a hard disk is a bad idea.

3. Are you an experienced typist with good keyboard skills? Yes No

If you don't like using a keyboard and would find remembering keystroke sequences difficult, or like the visual aspect of icons, then you are better off with an Apple machine or a word processor that uses Windows.

4. Do you need to combine your words with illustrations and lots of tables? Yes No

If so then you'll probably find Windows-based software or the Mac your best choice.

5. Do you find using modern technology easy? Yes No

Most modern day word processors claim to be user-friendly: that is, easy to use. But some are easier than others. As a general rule the more that a word processor can do the more complicated it will be to use, because you have more commands to remember. Some top of the range word processors have 240-250 features.

6. Do you need to ensure all your work is spelt correctly? Yes No

There can be few people who wouldn't find this a useful feature. However, some of the more basic word processors do not have a spell-checker as standard. Look and ask before buying. Some also use American spelling.

7. Do you need to count the number of words you write? Yes No

If you are a writer or journalist, knowing how many words you have written can be important in meeting an editor's brief. A word counter saves a lot of time, but not all word processing software has one.

8. Are you likely to be using other word processing software of a different type? Yes No

ASCII (pronounced Asskey) is the universal language of computers. If you can convert documents into this language then your document can be read by another word processor. This might be very useful if you share work with others, or perhaps have to work on other computers frequently. Not all word processors allow ASCII conversion or the 'import' and 'export' of work done on other word processors.

9. Will you need your word processor to do scientific things such as calculate numbers or use mathematical formulae? Yes No

Not all word processors can do this. Again check before buying.

10. Do you think that you might need frequent help while working on a document? Yes No

If so then a word processor with a good on-line help facility can be of benefit. With this you can just press a button and information will come up on the screen on what a particular command does and how to use it. To leave Help you just click on another button and you are back in your document. As with everything else, some Help functions are better than others.

11. Do you think you will need a lot of help and advice after you have bought your word processor? Yes No

Manufacturers of more expensive word processing software operate advice and support lines which you can telephone to ask for help. Many such manufacturers will also provide existing users with better, upgraded versions of their products at a cut price.

12. Will you need to prepare long or complicated documents? Yes No

A word processor with a built-in outliner might help you structure your work better. This lets you draw up a skeleton of headings and subheadings for any document you want to create, which you can then expand on using the word processor. See Chapter 11 for further information.

CASE STUDIES

Jane

As a student Jane is pretty strapped for cash, so she can't afford an expensive machine. In fact she is quite happy with a secondhand computer, which she manages to buy cheaply from another student. It's several years old, with a black and white monitor, it's not very fast and doesn't have a large memory. But that doesn't worry Jane. As far as she is concerned this computer will let her do the word processing that she wants.

She completes the package with an inexpensive bubblejet printer which her mother buys her as a present.

Full of excitement, she starts work on a college essay, which has to be 3,000 words long, but which she has put off starting. Now she can't delay any longer. She sits down in front of the word processor, but just can't think of anything to write. Every time she tries to come up with a good beginning her mind goes blank. In desperation she just starts anywhere, writing down anything that she can think of. Strangely enough, the more she writes the more thoughts keep popping into her head.

Very soon she begins to like this way of working because she doesn't need to get the order of her thoughts precisely right, not at first anyway. She can just plonk phrases, sentences and paragraphs down on the screen as they come, knowing that all this effort isn't wasted because she can move them around and put them in the right order later on. She doesn't have to bother about getting the spelling correct because she also knows that she can correct that later.

Jane is discovering one of the main advantages of word processing: that you need never waste any of your words because you can recycle them. Before using a word processor Jane would have written out notes on a sheet of paper, then written a first draft, then a second, and then probably a third one which she'd then hand in. All of the words she had written down for the notes and first drafts would be useless and thrown away.

Alex

Alex has come across a wonderful software package that he begins using on his word processor immediately – ready-made business letters. He has always had problems writing letters: he is never really sure what to say and spends ages agonising over the words, changing them constantly. But with this package he is able to load these ready-made letters into his word processor, adapt them accordingly and mail them out to his clients or would-be clients. The letters cover topics such as sales, debt collection, apologies and much, much more. Not only is this time-saving for Alex, but he is really beginning to discover the versatility of his word processor and computer.

Michael

Since he sees investing in computers and word processing as being of great importance, both short-term and long-term to his writing business, Michael buys two machines. For his choice of computer, Michael opts for a laptop machine that is about the size of an A4 pad of paper. It has the power of a standard PC, but he reckons that because of its small size and because it's battery operated he will be able to take it with him when he covers stories, so he can tap his words straight in without having to make handwritten notes which then have to be keyed in anyway later.

He also buys a standard desk-top machine which he will use for larger documents – such as books – which he works on at home.

3
Improving Your Keyboard Skills

The better your keyboard skills the faster you will be at word processing. And since the typewriter keyboard and that of the word processor are largely the same, if you are an experienced typist you should have few problems adjusting.

LEARNING TO TOUCH TYPE

You can of course type by using a couple of fingers to peck at the keys. Indeed, many people spend all their typing careers working in no other way, especially as 'two-fingered' typists can achieve quite a high typing speed. But using a keyboard in this 'natural' way is inefficient and prone to inaccuracy, largely because the eyes and fingers quickly get tired.

However, if you are going to use a keyboard for even just an hour a day then learning to touch type is certainly a sound investment. You should learn as soon as possible, particularly if you haven't typed before so you don't pick up any bad typing habits.

If you are a two fingered typist how many words can you type in a minute? How many mistakes do you make while doing this? Learning to touch type will help increase your typing speed and reduce the number of mistakes that you make.

Action Point

If I learned how to touch type, what writing tasks would I be able to perform faster?

1 . . . .

2 . . . .

3 . . . .

4 . . . .

5 . . . .

HOW LONG TO LEARN?

Learning the techniques of touch typing is relatively simple. It can take between 12 and 20 hours of reasonable effort, though to become a fast and competent typist capable of turning out 60 words a minute consistently takes a great deal more concentrated effort since speed builds up slowly.

However, after a few weeks of practice touch typing will become second nature to you and you'll be able to concentrate less and less on the keyboard and more and more on what you are typing and on using the full range of the word processor's commands and facilities.

There are a number of ways in which you can learn to touch type. Each has its advantages and disadvantages and can be chosen to suit your own temperament and circumstances.

- You can use **books** to teach yourself. There are a large number of touch typing books on the market, each with its own range of typing exercises of increasing complexity. These probably provide as good a starting point as any, especially if you are sufficiently motivated.

- For those who feel they might need the help and encouragement of a tutor, many local education authorities run **evening classes** in keyboard skills.

- Finally, a high tech alternative to the standard text book is **keyboard training software**. There are a number of such programs around.

Once you have committed yourself to improving your keyboard skills you must spend as long as you can at the keyboard itself.

CHECKLIST

1. Are you happy learning things on your own?
   (If yes then use typing books or software) Yes No

2. Do you need to be shown how to do something?
   (If yes then take a course) Yes No

3. Do you like to learn with others?
   (If yes then take a course) Yes No

4. Do you need the motivation that others provide?
   (If yes then take a course) Yes No

5. Are you self motivated?
   (If yes then use typing books or software) Yes No

6. Do you have privacy at home?
   (If no then take a course) Yes No

7. Do you have spare time at home?
   (If no then take a course) Yes No

8. Do you have a local education college nearby?
   (If no then use typing books or software) Yes No

ACTION POINTS

- Visit the local library and take out some books on touch typing.
- Contact the local education college and find out if they have any courses on keyboard skills. Look up their telephone number and write it here . . . .
- Identify a regular time each day when you could sit down to learn to touch type. When would that time be? Write it here . . . . . .
  . . . .
- Talk to people who can touch type already and ask them what difficulties they found, what benefits they gain from touch typing. Will they be prepared to give you some help? Make a list of those people here . . . .
  . . . .
  . . . .
  . . . .

CASE STUDIES

Jane

While she knows something about computers and modern technology and is learning more from her technical friends, Jane is still an absolute novice when it comes to keyboard skills. In fact she has never really typed in her life, except for a short computer course at school. Jane decides that an evening class is the best choice for her because there is one running at her college, and she finds she needs the motivation gained from working with others to be at her best. The course is quite useful though Jane finds that it goes a little slowly at first, because the tutor tends to wait for the slowest member of the class, which can be frustrating.

Alex

Alex, the accountant, is very definitely a two-fingered typist. He certainly doesn't feel he has time to attend classes; in any case the thought of being stuck in a room full of young women improving their secretarial skills fills him with a sense of dread and potential humiliation. He also decides that books are just going to clutter up his desk, and as he feels that he should embrace new technology wholeheartedly he decides to go for the tutorial software. This he finds easy to use, though some of the messages that come up on screen when he makes a mistake become a little tedious after a while. But he finds the automatic facility of the software to work out his typing speed and the number of mistakes he makes in a piece very useful.

Michael

Michael is well used to using a keyboard since he has to supply typewritten copy to editors all the time. So he has become an adept two-fingered typist and is not sure if he really needs to learn touch typing. In the end he decides that on the whole it would be better for him – if he is to make an investment in new technology then it's as good a time as any to update his skills.

Because he is something of a loner and of course loves books, Michael decides that this has to be the obvious way for him to learn. He asks his wife, who used to be a personal assistant, if she still has her old typing books. She hunts them down and, though they are a few years old, Michael finds that they are quite adequate to teach him keyboard skills for word processing, even though they are typing books. Now at the end of his working day he spends between 30 and 60 minutes going through the exercises. Some he finds far harder than others, especially with his history of fast two-fingered typing which leads him back into old ways time and time again. However, he perseveres and after five to six weeks he feels fairly confident about his new-found touch typing ability and experiences the pleasure and enjoyment of learning a totally new skill, something that he hasn't done for a number of years.

4
Healthy Word Processing

You can, of course, rush off and just begin word processing without any ill effects or doing any harm to yourself. After all, as a dangerous activity, word processing probably ranks somewhere down at the very bottom of the list alongside flower arranging and dominoes. However, that doesn't mean there aren't potential problems against which you should take adequate precautions. The number of high profile legal cases which have been brought against employers by computer operating employees illustrates the point.

So, while it's highly unlikely that you'll have any real problems unless you are doing a considerable amount of word processing, even if you are only spending short periods of time at the keyboard it is worth acquiring good techniques as early as possible. Then, if and when you start doing a lot more word processing you won't have formed any potentially damaging bad habits and you will automatically be doing the right things.

IDENTIFYING POTENTIAL PROBLEMS

Using bad word processing techniques for extended periods can affect the whole of your body, though the main areas that are likely to suffer are the shoulders and back, the wrists and arms, the eyes and the head. Which of these parts suffers most, if at all, will depend not only on the way that you behave at the keyboard, but also on the computer.

Rightly or wrongly, in recent years computers have been blamed for a number of complaints and health problems, including the following:

- There is evidence that prolonged periods in front of a VDU can aggravate existing **eye problems**. Eighty per cent of VDU users are thought to suffer from problems with their eyesight.

- According to some surveys, nearly one third of office workers who use VDUs are said to suffer from **eyestrain**, **tiredness** and **back, neck** and **shoulder pains**.

- About eight per cent of VDU users suffer from **rashes** and **skin problems** which appear two to four hours after starting work at a VDU, but tend to disappear overnight.

- The electrical and magnetic emissions from computers have been claimed to be responsible for **miscarriages** among pregnant women, though research results are contradictory.

- Probably the most worrying condition associated with word processing however is **repetitive strain injury** or RSI. This is caused by repeated and rapid movements of the arms, hands and fingers associated with typing. RSI inflames the tendons and muscles of the arms and when mild this soon disappears. However, when the condition is more severe the sufferer can quite literally be crippled for months or even years. Permanent injury can even be caused.

AVOIDING PROBLEMS BY SITTING CORRECTLY

Many of the problems listed above can be avoided or alleviated by simply sitting correctly at your word processor.

- When seated at your desk your feet should rest flat on the floor or on a footrest. This is particularly important if you suffer from back problems. Your thighs should be supported comfortably on the seat and there should be sufficient room on the seat for you to have movement of your hips so they aren't cramped.

- Make sure that the seat is adjusted so that you don't slump forward while you work. This can lead to tired shoulders, restricted breathing and poor digestion.

- You should shift your position constantly so that the pressure is temporarily removed from your spine, especially when you are spending a long time in front of the computer screen. If you can, avoid working in front of the computer for more than four or five hours a day. Also, take many short frequent breaks from typing and the screen and a break of 12-15 minutes every hour when you stretch out your arms and back.

Correct position for desk and chair.

- Position the keyboard on the desk so that when you type your forearms are roughly parallel to the floor. The angle between your forearm and upper arm should then be between 70 and 90 degrees.

- When sitting comfortably at your desk, the screen of the computer should be 35-60 cm away from you.

- Move the computer screen to the left and right, and if you can also up and down so that the sun and lights are not glaring on it, making you frequently shift your position in order to see. Ideally your computer should be at right angles to a window so you achieve an even spread of light on the desk and papers. If you sit with your back to the window you will either cast a shadow over the monitor, or have light reflected on it, which will make you squint. If you sit facing the window then you will not only be dazzled by the light, but also be more easily distracted by what is going on outside. Additionally your eyes will continually have to adjust from the brightness outside to the relatively dark interior of the room. Try to ensure that you work at your computer in a slightly dark room so your eyes aren't continually switching between a muted computer screen and a bright office.

- Try and create an open space beyond your desk into which you can let your eyes wander from time to time as this helps keep them relaxed.

- Try and ensure that the centre of the screen is so positioned that you look down on it from an angle of between 15 and 20 degrees.

- Make sure that the contrast of the computer screen isn't too harsh or the brightness too great. Experiment to find a happy medium. There are also two ways in which characters can be displayed on a computer screen: either dark characters on a light background or light characters on a dark background. The second of these is more restful on the eyes. Switch to it if your computer and software allow you to.

- If your word processor lets you, alter the size of the characters that appear on the screen, so that they are larger and more comfortable to see. Have your eyes checked by an optician regularly.

- Fit an anti-glare screen if you work in a room where the glare from overhead lighting is a problem and clean the screen frequently so that it is easy to see the characters.

CHOOSING THE RIGHT FURNITURE

Of considerable help in ensuring you sit in the correct position is having the right desk to put your word processor on. One of the main mistakes that novice and even experienced word processing users make is to spend many hours in front of a computer seated at a desk that is entirely wrong for word processing. Look for these features in choosing a desk for word processing.

- The desktop should be about 70 cm high, so that when seated at the keyboard your forearms are approximately parallel to the floor and your elbows angled between 70 and 90 degrees. You will probably have to experiment with the relative positions of the keyboard, desk and chair to achieve this. Traditional writing desks are often higher than 70cm which means that you can't achieve the right working position without lifting and hunching your shoulders.

- If you can, make sure that the surface of the desk is not shiny otherwise light will reflect off it into your eyes.

- The desk should also be deep enough (about 75 cm) to allow the keyboard and screen not to be so close to the front of it that they cause eyestrain. Ideally the screen should be somewhere between 35 and 60cm from your eyes. A deep desk also helps in stopping papers and books falling off the back. If you only have limited desk space then you should make sure that your computer has a small footprint, or use a system that can stand on the floor.

- A purpose-built computer desk with a pull-out keyboard shelf will help you achieve the correct posture.

- Of equal importance as the desk in helping you word process safely is the chair on which you sit. A good typist's chair is suitable since it can be adjusted for height and position, and also provides support for your lower back. For added comfort the seat should be covered with a porous material that absorbs sweat. If you don't think you sweat a great deal from this area of your anatomy then try sitting on a plastic seated chair on a sunny day!

HEALTHY EXERCISES

Word processing involves sitting in the same position for long periods, but you can help yourself by performing a series of exercises before you start work at the keyboard, or at any time during the day.

Exercising your hands and arms

1. Sit at your desk and put your forearms flat on the desktop with the palms facing downwards. Then turn your palms upwards then turn them palm down again. Repeat this exercise 20 times.

2. Put your forearms on the desk top with palms down and with your hands and fingers straight out in front of you. Spread your fore-finger away from your middle finger, then bring them together. Repeat this 20 times. Do this for every pair of fingers on each hand.

3. Holding your hands in front of you touch the tip of each finger to the tip of your thumb. Do this five times on each hand.

4. Hold your arms out in front of you with the palms facing downwards. Keeping your fingers straight bend each wrist so that the tips of fingers are pointing at the ground. Then bend your wrists backwards so that the finger tips point to the sky. Do this ten times for each wrist.

Exercising your neck and shoulders

1. Sit in a straight-backed chair with your shoulders lifted. Relax your neck and lower your chin until it rests on your chest. Then slowly raise it to its original position. Do this five times.

2. Still sitting in the chair, bend your head to the left, slowly bring it right till it is central again and then bend it to the right. Repeat five times each side.

3. Either sitting or standing shrug your shoulders moving them forward as your shoulders rise, then moving them backwards as the shoulders go down so that you are making a circular motion. Do this ten times.

Exercising your back

1. Stand up and straighten your arms behind your back. Clasp your hands together, then gently raise your hands, still keeping your arms as straight as possible. Go as far as you comfortably can then lower. Repeat five times.

2. Still standing, put your hands in the small of your back and then move your hips forward so that your lower back curls slightly. Hold that position for a count of five, then gently return to the original position. Do this three to five times.

ACTION POINTS

- Visit office furniture show rooms and discover what furniture is available. Try the furniture out.

- Begin looking through office furniture and equipment catalogues for suitable chairs and desks. Start sending for catalogues through the post.

- Make a list of the main points concerning correct posture and technique and stick this to the desk near your word processor. It will act as a reminder to you.

CHECKLIST

Your computer

Is your computer screen large enough? (At least 12 inches across)	Yes	No
Is your keyboard connected to the system unit by a lead so it can be moved around, rather than attached to the system unit in a way that means it can't be moved?	Yes	No
Does your VDU have contrast and darkness control?	Yes	No
Can you tilt and swivel your VDU?	Yes	No
Can the characters and images on your screen be clearly seen?	Yes	No
Is your screen clear from flicker?	Yes	No
Does your VDU screen show light coloured characters on a dark background, rather than the other way around?	Yes	No
Is there an anti-glare filter fitted to your screen?	Yes	No
Is your keyboard comfortable to use and the keys positive in their action?	Yes	No
Is your VDU positioned at right angles to the window?	Yes	No
Is there an open space beyond the VDU for you to face?	Yes	No

Your desk

Is the top of your desk large enough for all the papers you need *and* your keyboard?	Yes	No

Is there room to place the papers and books you need on either side of your VDU?	Yes	No
Is your desk deep enough (at least 75cm deep) so that you can move back the VDU to a comfortable distance?	Yes	No
Do you have enough leg room under the desk?	Yes	No
Does the top of your desk have a matt finish so light doesn't reflect off it?	Yes	No
Is there a footrest?	Yes	No

Your chair

Does your chair have a five-star base to make it more stable?	Yes	No
Can you adjust the height of your seat?	Yes	No
Can you adjust the backrest?	Yes	No
Can your chair swivel?	Yes	No
Is the chair covered in a porous fabric?	Yes	No

If you answered No to any of these questions, then try to rectify the situation for your own safety and comfort.

CASE STUDIES

Jane

Jane hasn't been word processing for many weeks before she begins to suffer from a few aches around her fingers and also some tiredness in her shoulders. At first, she doesn't know what is causing the problem, though she does find that it seems to be worse in the evenings when she's been doing some word processing. She finds this surprising as she hasn't really been spending a long time at the keyboard. But then a friend who works as a secretary drops by and sees how she is working. Jane has her word processor on a student's desk, which is OK for writing on, but doesn't have the depth for word processing, so that the keyboard barely fits in front of the monitor. The result? Jane's forearms and wrists get no support at all, so they tire very quickly. In that position it's no surprise that Jane has been having wrist and hand problems, the real surprise is that she hasn't been getting headaches or tired eyes from looking at the screen from such a short distance. The problem is resolved by Jane turning her desk around so that she sits at the narrow end and looks down the desk at the screen. It's not an ideal solution, but it's better than before.

Michael

Having learned how to touch type and having built up a respectable speed at the keyboard, Michael is now a fully fledged word processing fan, spending more and more time at the keyboard — particularly when the creative juices are going and he doesn't like to break away and spoil the flow. One morning when Michael goes to the keyboard he finds that within one or two sentences he is suffering quite severe shooting pains up and down his arms. These disappear when he stops typing but come back as soon as he starts again. Michael doesn't know it, but he is suffering from the initial symptoms of RSI.

Of course he half suspects that the keyboard is to blame and so does a little research on the subject. His reading shows him that there is nothing the matter with how he has the computer, desk and chair set up. The problem is simply caused by him spending too long at any one time typing. The solution is simple – take frequent breaks. Michael gives his sore arms a few days to rest, then starts word processing again. With his new routine of plenty of breaks the pain no longer troubles him. And to get over the problem of having to stop in mid-flow he invests in a small portable tape recorder. Now if he feels he has to take a rest, he can still be creative by speaking into the recorder.

5
Starting Word Processing

By now you should have a good idea of what a word processor actually does and whether word processing is going to be of use to you. You should also have a fair idea of what to look for when buying word processing equipment; know where to go for help in learning keyboard skills; and how to make sure that you don't end up with painful conditions that make you wish you'd stuck with your pen. Now it's time to find out what a word processor actually can do.

There are literally hundreds of word processors around, from the cheap and simple through to the expensive and comprehensive, each with their own particular ways of working. Not only that, but as you've already read in Chapter 2, there are several different ways of operating word processors using the keyboard, menus or a mouse. Because of this, *How to Start Word Processing* can only sensibly cover the principles of word processing and not the specifics. For more detailed information about how a particular word processor works you should consult its manual.

USING THE KEYBOARD

If you are used to typing you might think that it is pretty straightforward to use the keyboard, and it is. But you need to know a few additional things about a word processor's keyboard, which is a little different from the one you find on a manual or even electronic typewriter.

Using the character keys

The most common form of word processing keyboard is a QWERTY keyboard, and is the one that you will have used if you have ever typed before. It is named after the first six letters of the top line of letter keys. These six letters, along with all the other letters of the alphabet, numbers between 0 and 9, and all the punctuation marks, are known as the character keys. They are laid out in four lines (see Fig.2).

The character keys make up the majority of the keyboard. If you press any of them once their character appears once on screen. If you hold the key down the character will be repeated on screen like this:

pppppppppppppppppppppppppppppppppppppppppppppppppppppppp

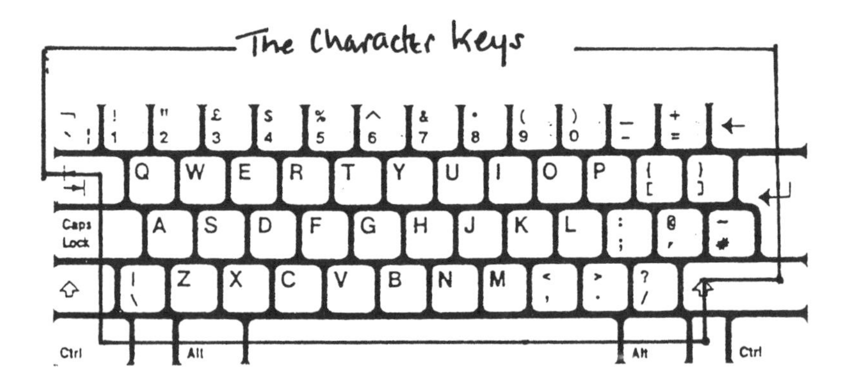

Fig. 2. The character keys.

Turning letters into capitals

As on a standard typewriter there is a **Shift** key. This key lets you 'shift' between upper and lower case characters. You will find one on either side of the character keys on a word processor's keyboard.

On the left hand side of the character keys you will also find another larger key, the **Caps Lock** key. When you press this it will 'lock' you into upper case. So if you type the alphabet with the Caps Lock off you will type:

abcdefghijklmnopqrstuvwxyz

and with Caps Lock on you will type:

ABCDEFGHIJKLMNOPQRSTUVWXYZ

You will type like this as long as the Caps Lock key is pressed down. A

Caps Lock indicator light will shine on the keyboard when the key is depressed.

Separating words

At the very bottom of the keyboard, running beneath the character keys, is the **Space Bar**. This is a long key about 5 inches (13 centimetres) in length. It doesn't type characters, but adds spaces. You would use the space bar to put a space between words, just as in this sentence.

Adding lines

Now we come to a rather special key, the **Enter** or **Return** key. This is a large L-shaped key found to the right of the character keys. It does partly the same job as on a standard typewriter keyboard by moving you to the next line. However, on the word processor this key has another job, because it is often used to tell your computer that you are ready for it to perform the command you have selected. In this respect it is the start button for a command.

This is the layout of the keys looked at so far. Used together they allow you to type in letters, numbers, punctuation marks and spaces, move down a line and shift between upper case and lower case letters, while the Enter key executes a chosen command or moves you down a line.

Using the rest of the keyboard

Until now there has been little difference between the keyboard of a typewriter and that of a word processor. All of that now changes because the remaining keys on the keyboard are rather special to the word processor. There are quite a number of these and you will have to know what they are before you can begin to word process successfully.

The key at the very top left hand corner of the keyboard has Esc written on it, which stands for **Escape**. This key lets you escape from what you are doing, either because you have changed your mind or realise that you have made a mistake. Some word processors and systems as well as having an Escape have an **Undo** command which will allow you to leave an operation when you are half way through it, with no damage done.

HOW TO 'PROCESS' YOUR WORDS

You will find 12 keys marked F1-F12 either to the right of the Escape key along the top of the keyboard or in two columns of six to the left of the character keys.

The F stands for 'Function' and not surprisingly these are known as the **Function** keys. Unlike the character keys they do not enter letters, digits or punctuation marks on the screen, but activate commands. You will use them to help you 'process' the text you create. Different function keys activate different commands on different word processing packages, so you will have to consult your manual to find out what each actually does. You will learn more about the function keys and what they can be used for in later chapters. Remember, these keys do not exist on a conventional typewriter.

Some other special keys are also only found on a computer keyboard. These are the **Ctrl** and **Alt** keys. They are located in pairs on either side of the character keys. The abbreviations stand for Control and Alternative. Because they are generally used in conjunction with other keys to perform special word processing operations, if you press them alone nothing will happen. By using these keys together with the function keys you are able to treble the number of commands you can issue. Again these operations vary from word processor to word processor.

For example, pressing the F1 can give one command, pressing F1 together with Ctrl a second command and pressing F1 with Alt a third command, all from that one F1 key.

To show that two keys have to be pressed simultaneously to issue a command a + is written between the two. Alt + F1 means that you must press the Alt and F1 keys together. You can also issue commands by pressing one key followed by another. This is written down without the +. For example, Alt F1.

Having looked at all these additional keys, you now have the word processing keyboard which looks something like Fig. 3.

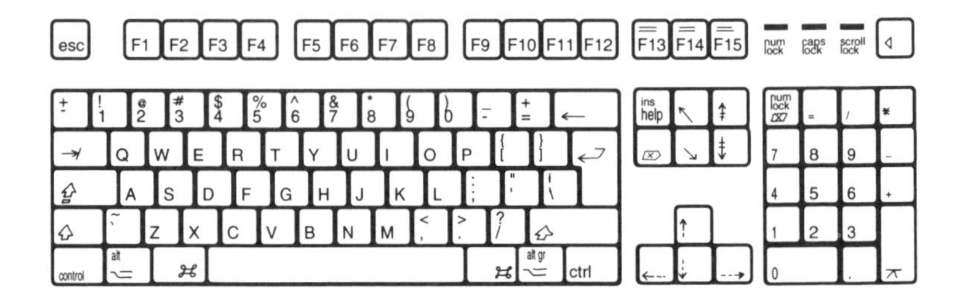

Fig. 3. The expanded keyboard.

WRITING WITH THE WORD PROCESSOR

Now you know something about the word processor keyboard it's time to start actually using the word processor.

Essentially a word processor has only two modes, or ways of working — you can either write words onto the screen or issue commands that tell the word processor what you want it to do with the words you've written.

The rest of this chapter will concentrate on writing words on the screen.

Writing on the screen

When you switch on many word processors, the first thing you will see is the **editing screen**. If you think of the keyboard as being the equivalent of an electronic pen, then the editing screen of the word processor is like the electronic equivalent of a sheet of writing paper.

The exact nature and design of this editing screen depends again upon the particular word processor you are using. With some this screen is virtually empty of information, while others contain more detail.

Fig. 4. shows the screen for the word processor WordPerfect.

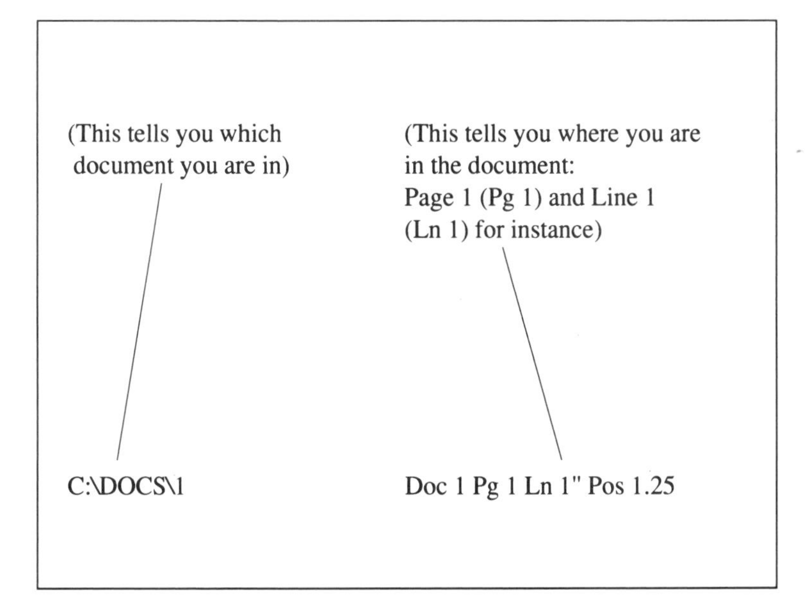

Fig. 4. A typical status line on an editing screen.

The information at the foot of the screen tells you the name of the document you are working on and your location in it. A document, by the way, is merely a piece of word processing work. It can be a single word, a letter or a book chapter for instance.

Whether you want to keep on-screen information to a minimum (so that it seems you are working as much as possible on a blank sheet of paper) or not depends upon your personal preference, something that you will discover as you try out more and more word processing packages.

Marking your place

No matter whether they contain a lot of information or only a little, all word processor screens have one thing in common: a small block of light blinking away. This is known as a **cursor**. Its exact size and shape

Fig. 5. You can set lefthand, righthand and top and bottom margins.

may vary between different computers and word processors. With some word processors the cursor always stays the same size, but with others it becomes larger when you activate certain commands.

The purpose of the cursor is to mark your place on the screen. It is the point at which all the letters, numbers and punctuation marks you type will appear.

Every time you switch on the word processor the cursor will be at the top left hand corner of the screen. Although you can position the cursor anywhere on the screen you want, in most circumstances you will set margins at the top, bottom and sides of the screen in which the cursor will not go and you cannot type (see Fig. 5).

Moving to the right

You can move the cursor upwards, downwards and sideways on the screen by using a variety of keys, the first of which you have already come across, the Space Bar. Press this once and the cursor moves one space to the right. Keep pressing the Space Bar down and the cursor will keep travelling right quite quickly across the screen.

Moving down the page

If you now type some letters or numbers you will see that they appear just behind the cursor on the same line. Now if you keep on typing, when the cursor reaches the end of the line it suddenly jumps down to the beginning of the next line. It will do this every time you reach the end of a line. If you are used to working with a typewriter you will know that you have to hit the Return key to move to the start of the next line. The word processor does this automatically. There is also no 'ding' of a bell which you get with a typewriter to warn you that you are nearing the end of a line.

This ability of your word processor to move automatically to the next line is known as **wordwrap** or **wraparound**, because you literally wrap one line of text round to the next. Wordwrap does away with the need for a carriage return at the end of line.

Starting a paragraph

Of course, you don't have to wait until you reach the end of a line before going on to the next one. Any time you want you can move to the next line by pressing the Enter key. For instance, you might want to do this when you are at the end of a paragraph in a letter or report. Then you would simply hit Enter once which would take you down to the next line, but as you want to leave a line of space between paragraphs you hit Enter once again, as shown below:

> This is how you start a new paragraph. [Press Enter]
> [Press Enter]
> Now you start your new paragraph here.

When your word processor wordwraps it issues something called a **soft return** at the end of the line. However, when you press Enter to go down to the end of the line the word processor issues what is known as a **hard return**. For now just remember the terms in case you come across them.

STARTING TO TYPE

When you are in the editing screen, as you press a character key that character will appear on screen and as you hit more keys the line of text will grow. As you've seen, the word processor automatically moves down to the next line when the previous line is full.

When the cursor reaches the very end of the last line of text on the screen as it pops down to the next line, the very top line of text at the top of the screen vanishes to make way for the new one at the bottom. This happens every time you move onto a new line at the bottom of the page (see Fig 6).

The novice word processor user may be startled when lines of text suddenly disappear. Don't worry. The text at the top of the page hasn't been lost, it's still there. It has been remembered by the computer but temporarily kept out of sight as the word processor gives you more 'paper' to write on. Because it is quite small the screen can generally only show you part of your document at any one time.

If you like, think of the screen as a picture frame placed in front of a roll of wallpaper several feet wide and several hundred feet long. By looking through the picture frame you can see only the piece of paper you are working on, but you can move the frame around to see other parts of the paper (see Fig. 7).

When you begin work on a new document the picture frame will be at the top left of the paper and you won't be able to move it further upwards or to the left. This is the very top of the document.

SUMMARY

- Characters you type on the keyboard appear on screen just behind the cursor.

- When you reach the end of a line you move automatically down to the next one. There is no need to press the Enter or Return key.

- When you are at the bottom of the screen adding a new line of text moves the top line of text out of sight. This is no problem as the text is not lost.

- You can easily move around a document to see more of it.

Line 1	Even the largest monitor screen can only
2	display so many lines of text on it at any
3	one time. So what happens to a document
4	that has more lines on it than can be
5	displayed on screen? Well, all that happens
6	is that the line of text at the top of the
7	screen moves upwards so that you can start
8	typing on a fresh line at the bottom of

Line 2	display so many lines of text on it at any
3	one time. So what happens to a document
4	that has more lines on it than can be
5	displayed on screen? Well, all that happens
6	is that the line of text at the top of the
7	screen moves upwards so that you can start
8	typing on a fresh line at the bottom of
9	the screen. Just like this.

Fig. 6 Scrolling down a document: the top line of text disappears as the cursor moves down to a fresh line at the bottom.

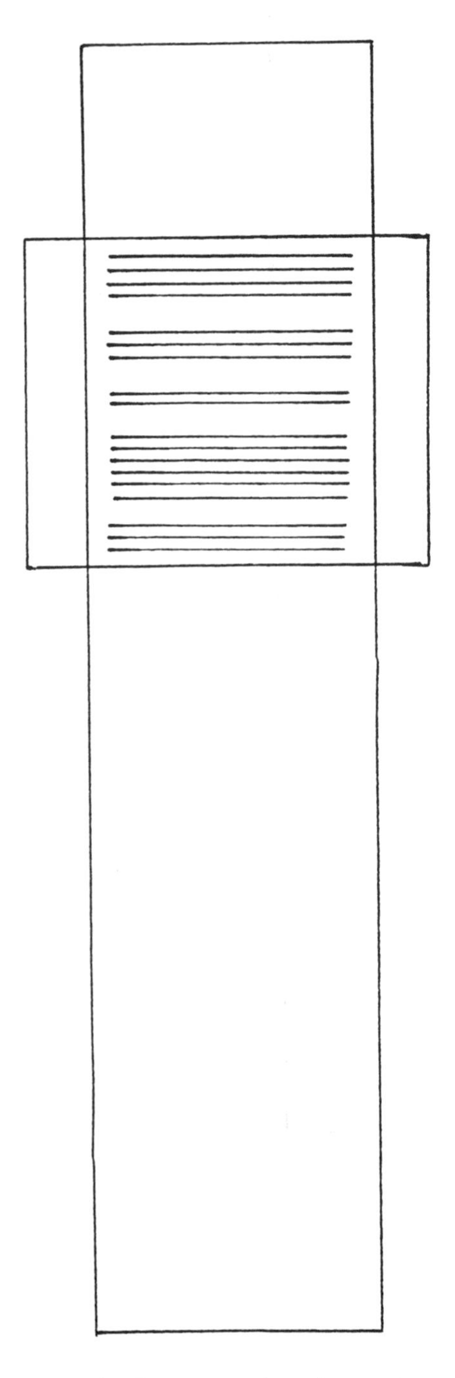

Fig. 7. Moving through a document: on long documents you can only see a small portion of it at any one time.

CASE STUDIES

Jane

Jane's word processor is quite difficult for her to use. The main problem is that she often has to use quite complicated combinations of keys to issue commands, which she keeps on forgetting. Some word processors come with a printed template which can be stuck over the top of the function keys showing at a glance what each one does. Jane's doesn't. The problem is made worse because the word processor she has been using at evening class is different from the one she has at home, so she has two command systems to memorise. In the end she solves the problem by writing out all the commands onto a sheet of paper which she tapes to the desk next to the keyboard.

Alex

Alex wants to get as much out of his word processor as quickly as possible, and though curious about just what the software can do, he practises assiduously, becoming adept and skilful at employing the most common and useful commands. These are the ones that he'll be using 70-80 per cent of the time, even when he becomes an experienced word processing user. At this early stage there is little benefit to Alex in spending many hours becoming an ace at paragraph numbering or making footnotes if he is going to use this less than once in a blue moon.

Pam

As an ex-typist, Pam has a different problem. The many hours she has spent typing have left her with a habit that is not at all good for word processing. Every time she reaches the end of a line her natural instinct is to press the Enter key, just as she would the return key of a typewriter. Only through a lot of practice does she finally break the habit.

Michael

Having his precious words disappear off the screen is difficult for Michael to cope with at first. 'I know that I can get the words back', he tells his wife, 'but I have to keep on checking, just to make sure they *are* there.' This problem is not an unusual one. Just keep thinking that the words are on that roll of paper which you can roll or unroll just as you wish.

6
Changing Your Mind

This chapter looks at how you can move around through the letter, essay or report you've typed and change it when you find a mistake or simply want to edit it.

MOVING AROUND A DOCUMENT

You've already seen that the cursor automatically moves around the screen when:

- new characters are typed in
- the space bar is pressed
- the end of a line is reached
- the Enter key is pressed.

But moving around a word processed document, such as a letter, report, or book, can be done in several other ways. The first of these is by using what are known as the **cursor keys**.

These are found to the right of the character keys, either in a block of keys numbered zero to nine or in a block of four keys between the character keys and the numbered keys. They are marked with arrows. The direction of the arrow indicates which way the cursor will move when the key is pressed. For instance, the key marked → moves the cursor one space to the right, while the key marked ← moves the cursor one space to the left.

The key marked ↑ moves the cursor up one line (unless you are on the top line of the document when the cursor will stay where it is). The key marked ↓ moves the cursor down one line each time it is pressed (unless you are on the bottom line of the document when the cursor will stay where it is).

However, if you press and hold down the up (↑) or down (↓) keys the cursor continues to move quickly up or down through the document. Moving the cursor like this is called **scrolling**. It allows you to move speedily upwards and downwards through a document.

When you press the cursor keys you move the cursor **over** letters and words that have already been typed on screen without moving or changing them in any way.

You can often use the cursor keys together with other keys; such as Ctrl, to move to the start of the next word in a line. For example Ctrl + → would move the cursor to the start of the next word to the right, while Ctrl + ← would move the cursor to the start of the first word to the left.

Moving around faster

There are four other keys which you can use to move more quickly around the editing screen. You'll find them next to the cursor keys.

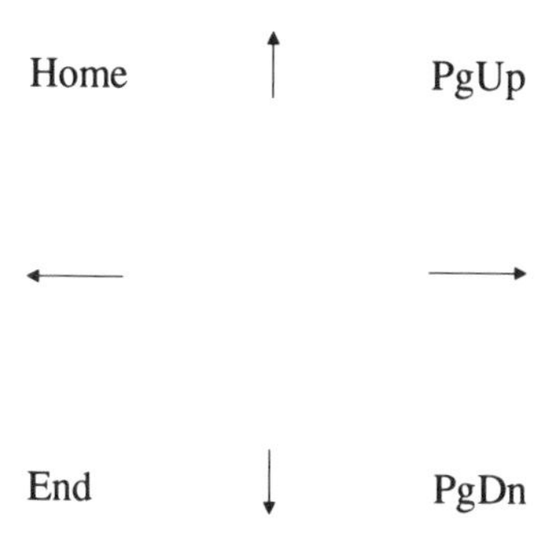

These keys are the **Home**, **End**, **PgUp** and **PgDn** keys. They let you move not just one line or character at a time, but over whole lines and pages at a time. Exactly how they do this varies between word processors, but for instance:

- the Home key can move the cursor either to the beginning of the line it's on or to the beginning of the document
- the End key can move the cursor either to the end of the line it's on or to the end of the document

- the PgUp (Page Up) key can move the cursor to the start of the previous page

- the PgDn (Page Down) key can move the cursor to the start of the next page.

There is one more key that helps you move the cursor around the screen. This is the **Tab** key. You will find it to the left of the character keys. The Tab key is marked something like this:

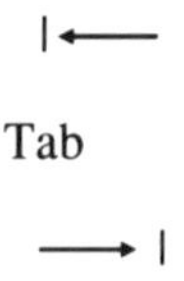

It does a similar job to the space bar only it moves the cursor to the right not just one space at time, but a number of spaces. You can set the number of spaces that you want it to move with each press. You might want to use the tab key to indent the first line of a paragraph, or to make sure that the characters you type stay in columns. For example, for his accountancy work, Alex finds the Tab key very useful because it lets him produce columns of figures, by making sure that the numbers (and even their decimal points) stay in a vertical line.

Going to a particular point

One other way remains to move around a document. When working on a long document you will often want to go to a particular point in a document as fast as possible. Most word processors have a **Go To** command that lets you do this. You can tell the word processor to go to a particular page, a line in the document, a 'marker' that you have previously put in the document or to a different document if you have split the screen into windows.

CHANGING YOUR WORK

If all you typed onto the screen was just as you wanted, you wouldn't have to make any changes. But this is the real world and even the most experienced typist makes mistakes now and then. However, a word processor lets you correct your mistakes quickly and easily, changing and removing them as and when you want. There are several ways that you can do this.

Inserting a character

Generally most word processors stay in what is known as **insert mode**. This allows you to insert a character into the text at the position of the cursor.

You can use the Insert mode to type in a missing letter. For instance, if you type 'rage' instead of 'range' you simply move the cursor using the cursor keys until it's on the 'g', then press 'n'. Hey presto, the 'n' appears between the 'a' and the 'g' and you have the word 'range'. The 'g' moves to the right to make room for the new character. All other characters to the right of the cursor also move right one space.

Erasing a character

But what if you have typed 'range' instead of 'rage', how do you remove that mistaken 'n'? There are three ways in which you can do that with a word processor.

1. At the right end of the top row of character keys (where the numbers are) keyboard you'll see the **Backspace** key. It looks like this:

   ←—— Backspace

   If you press it, the cursor will move one space to the left erasing any character it finds there.

2. At the bottom and to the far right of the keyboard, is another erasing key. This is marked **Del** which stands for Delete. When you press it the character beneath the cursor is erased. In the example given here, you would have to position the cursor over the 'n' in 'range' and then press Del to get 'rage'.

   With both the Backspace and Delete keys you'll see that when you erase a character, all the characters to the right of it shuffle left to fill the space left by the erased character.

3. The final method of erasing a character uses a large key at the bottom right of the keyboard below the cursor keys. It is marked **Ins**. When this is 'on' you are in Insert mode, which allows you to insert a character into a word. But if Insert is 'off' then your word processor inserts new text at the same time as it erases old text – in other words it types over your mistake.

   For example, if you have totally messed up a word by writing 'range' instead of 'panda' then you would just position the cursor on the 'r' of range, press Ins, then type 'panda'. Instead of characters to the right of the cursor moving they stay where they are and the character beneath the cursor is replaced by a new one.

This is known as **overtyping** and is a very useful means of erasing existing text quickly and replacing it with new. You should always take care when overtyping because it's very easy to erase text that you wanted to keep, or to press the Insert command unintentionally and do the same. When you are adding new text to the end of a document you will notice no difference between Overtyping and Insert modes because there are no words there to overtype.

Summary

- The Backspace key moves the cursor to the left and it erases any characters that it meets.
- The Del (Delete) key erases the character on which the cursor stands.
- When the Insert key is on you can insert characters into other words without erasing any characters.
- When the Insert key is off you are in Overtype. This allows you to type directly onto existing characters without having to erase them first.

SAVING YOUR WORK

Having gone to all the trouble of creating a document you will want to keep it. Any work that you do on your word processor is stored initially in the computer's short-term memory. This only remembers information as long as there is electrical power to the computer.

When a document is stored here it is very vulnerable. If the power to the computer fails at this stage all of your work will be lost. It doesn't matter whether the document amounts to just a line or two or 30 or 40 pages, all of it will go – forever. Then all of the time, effort and thought you have put in to writing it will be wasted, absolutely. Computers are not sentimental about things like this.

Unfortunately the power supply to the computer can be lost all too easily: storms or electrical problems can turn off the power to your home or office; your computer can blow a fuse; another appliance can blow a fuse and the mains; or you can just be absent minded and turn off the computer without thinking.

Imagine if any of these happened when you were on the last page of an essay that had to be submitted in just 30 minutes, or you were working on a quotation for a new client and were desperately late already.

For all of the advantages of word processing it does have one major disadvantage. There is no record of the work you have done if things go wrong as you'll have no written notes or first draft to refer to.

Therefore it is vital that you learn to **save your work regularly** to the computer's internal hard disk or on to a floppy disk. When a document is stored there it can be stored more permanently.

Naming your work

When you save a document on your word processor for the first time the word processor will ask you to **name** it. Unfortunately you can't call it anything you want. Instead, you must conform to a standard format and certain rules. Generally file names must have three parts to them. A name, a full stop and a file extension.

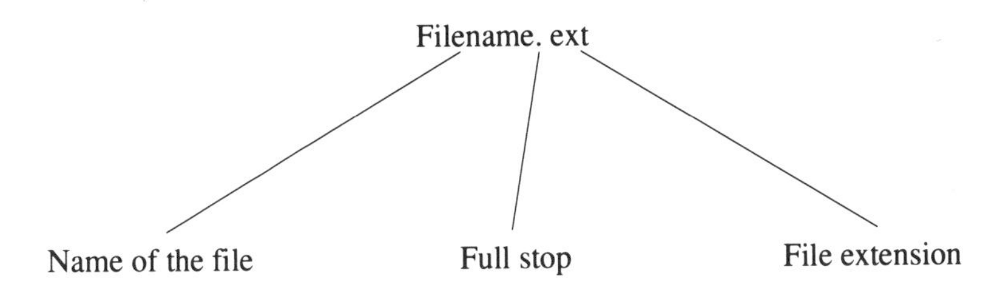

The name can be up to eight characters in length, which can be any combination. You can use letters and/or numbers and letters can be either in upper or lower case. You can also use certain punctuation marks, though not all. So, rather than trying to remember what you can and cannot use, it's easier to use just letters and numbers for your document names. Whatever combination of characters you use there must be no spaces between them.

You do not need to give your files a file extension. Your word processor will do this automatically (probably something like DOC or WRl), but you can add an extension of your own, for instance INV for invoice or ART for article. If you don't give your file a file extension you don't have to include a full stop after the name. If you do add your own file extension then you will need to add a full stop. These are good file names:

A

A.DOC

ABCDEFGH.DOC

12345678.DOC

ABCD5678.DOC

AbCdEfGh.doc

ABCDefgh.inv

These are bad file names:

ABCDEFGHIJ
(too many letters – you can only have up to eight)

abcdefghdoc
(no full stop between name and extension – there must be one)

abc defg.doc
(a space has been left – there can't be one)

Once you have given a document a name you do not have to type in the document's name again when you save it. However, each time you save the document you have the choice to save it under another name, as long as it conforms to the rules above. You might want to save the document under another name if you want two different versions of it.

Though the above rules apply to most computer systems, some differ in particular respects. For example, Apple Macs allow you to use file names that are up to 32 characters in length.

Checklist

Begin thinking of file names for documents that are appropriate to your business, college work, or personal life. Keep checking the rules above.

Think of ten names for documents that you might find everyday life.

1. . . . .
2. . . . .
3. . . . .
4. . . . .
5. . . . .
6. . . . .
7. . . . .
8. . . . .
9. . . . .
10. . . . .

Saving long files

Some word processors let you save files of any length, while others set a limit. The word processor's manual will tell you which method your word processor uses. However, even if your word processor lets you save a file of any size, there are advantages in keeping the size of your documents quite small. For a start, if you have a large file it will always take the computer longer to retrieve and save it than it will a shorter one. Second, it can be very inconvenient working on a long file because you can lose your way around, wasting time trying to find the section you want. Third, some word processors simply don't like long files and can end up corrupting and damaging them.

If you are tempted to save a really long document ask yourself whether you need to work in a document of that length. Is there a convenient and appropriate way of dividing up the document, perhaps into chapters, different sections of a report or categories? A good comfortable file length is about 5,000 words.

Saving your work regularly

While you are working on a document save it regularly, say **every 20 minutes** or so. It is better to be safe than sorry and the time you actually lose in saving is nothing compared to the amount of time you would lose having to re-key in even just a page or two of text.

If you are going to perform a powerful command on a document t[illegible] work first, then you can always retrieve it if the command [illegible]ong.

Bac[illegible] the work on your hard disk onto floppies at the end of every day, or at least every week. Your manual will tell you how to do this. This may seem inconvenient at first, but it is far better than losing all your work. This is particularly important if you are working on a large project, such as a book or work for clients, on which your livelihood depends. Storing information on floppy disk is also a sensible precaution in the event of anything going wrong with your word processor program or the computer, such as a faulty hard drive. Then at least you will be able to use your floppy disks on another machine, at least temporarily.

If you don't want to save your work onto floppies at the end of every day then make sure you have a printout on paper of the work that you have done.

When you have saved your work onto floppy disks then keep them away from the computer, preferably in another room, so that if anything serious happens, such as a fire, then they stand a better chance of being safe.

When you store your files on floppies, make a list of the files that are on there with a brief description of their content; you will save a great deal of time hunting for documents if you ever need to find work on them in a few months' time. Store your floppies in disk boxes specially made for the purpose.

You should also make copies on floppy disk of all your word processing software as soon as you buy it and do not use it for everyday work.

STARTING WORK ON ANOTHER DOCUMENT

When saving your work you can save it either to your hard disk or to a floppy and keep your document on the screen (you will want to do this if you are going to continue working on the document); or you can save it but ask the word processor to remove it from the screen (you would do this if you wanted to work on another document).

If you clear the screen you can either create a new piece of work by typing on it or retrieve a document that you've already created from the hard or floppy disk.

Retrieving work you've already saved is easy: your word processor has a **Retrieve** command which will present you with a list of documents that you've previously created. You choose which you want and

then call it up. Alternatively you can type in the name o[illegible]
that you want. The file will then appear on screen.

FINDING YOUR WORK EASILY

Even after only a few weeks of word processing you could have saved a large number of files, all about different things and relating to different subjects. This may not be too much of a problem when you are storing all of your documents on floppy disk because all you have to do is keep files on related subjects together on one disk.

However, you have a major problem when all your files are stored on a hard disk. This stores so much information that if you didn't have an organised filing system it would be like dropping all your files and documents into a great big sack through which you had to hunt every time you wanted a particular file. That would waste a lot of time and effort because you would have to look at every file name to find the right one.

Creating places to keep your work

Therefore, as with any good filing system, it's sensible to keep similar documents together. You can do this with a word processor by grouping documents into particular places on the hard disk, known as **directories**.

Directories can be as big as you like and you can create them for whatever documents you like. For example, you could make a directory for PERSONAL matters, another directory for WORK, and another for COLLEGE. The choice is yours. Each directory has a name which follows the same principle and rules as for naming files, that is they can have up to eight characters, but they don't have file extensions.

Having created one directory you can then create other directories within it, which is known as a sub-directory. This is rather like having a folder of work within another folder. For instance, you might want to create a directory that contains all of the information on your clients, but then further divide this into sub-directories for CLIENT LETTERS, CLIENT INVOICES, CLIENT PROPOSALS, or anything else that's appropriate. You could even divide these sub-directories into further sub-directories for each client. That would give you a directory structure that looked like Fig. 8.

The directory structure shows that the user has created four main directories: Accounts, Letters, Clients and Marketing. These are divided [illegible] ories. For example, the Clients directory is divided into thre [illegible] ectories. Each contains work for three different clients 1, 2 and [illegible]

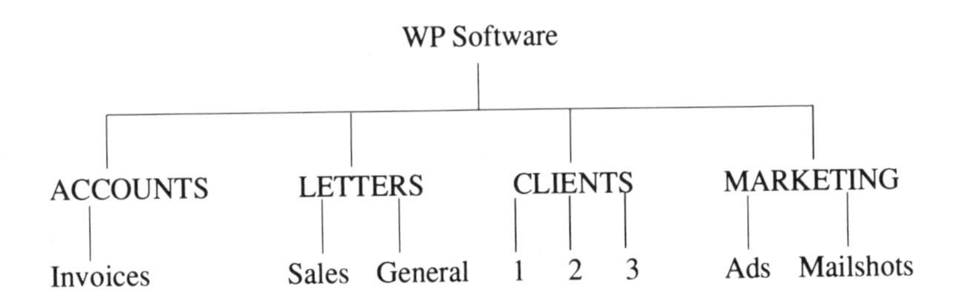

Fig. 8. A sample directory structure.

By following the directory system you can have files with the same names, but in different directories. Without the directory set up every file you saved would have to have a different name.

However, when you set up any directory structure like this, you can't just go to a document: you have to use the right route to reach it. In computer terms this route is known as a file 'path'. There is such a path to every file that you save on your hard drive and you can either reach it by typing in a file path or by calling up the appropriate directory and selecting from the list of file names.

ACTION POINTS

What directories will you need for your personal needs, for work, education or leisure. Begin listing them here.

1. . . . .
2. . . . .
3. . . . .
4. . . . .
5. . . . .
6. . . . .
7. . . . .
8. . . . .

Begin organising these directories into a tidy structure of directories and sub-directories. Draw it on a sheet of paper.

HIDING YOUR DOCUMENTS

Once you have written a document you might want to make certain that no one else has access to it – particularly if you are sharing a computer and word processor with other people. This may be because you keep confidential information on your word processor or because you want to stop someone accidentally, or intentionally, changing or erasing a document that you've created. You can do this by giving a document a **password** which the word processor will ask for when you try to retrieve a document. Unless the other person knows what the password is they won't be able to get in.

The only problem with this is that you must not forget the password or you won't be able to retrieve the document either. For that reason you should make the password something that is memorable to you. You can always change the password later if you think that someone else has discovered it.

TIDYING UP YOUR WORD PROCESSOR

From time to time you should keep a check on the amount of space you have remaining on your disks. Even large hard disks fill up quickly when you are working hard, especially if you are taking back ups of your files. If you don't regularly check the available space then you might find that you don't have enough space to save the file you are working on. This means that you might have to exit the document without being able to save any of it, which would be a great waste of your time and effort.

What is more, if you do try and save a document when there isn't enough room you can scramble the information already on your disk, so that some of it is lost, corrupted or made very difficult to retrieve. Therefore you should try and make sure that a good proportion of your floppy or hard disk – perhaps 20 to 30 per cent – is kept as spare capacity. You should never be tempted to fill them right to the brim. The directory command will be able to tell you just how much space is available to you.

You can make sure that you always have space on your hard disk by periodically going through all the directories on your hard disk and identifying unneeded files which you can erase. Files can be removed from your word processor by using its Delete file command. The word processor will ask you to confirm that you want to do this and then obey if you say yes.

If you think that there is a possibility that you may need that document again then copy it over to a floppy disk (your word processor manual will tell you how to do this), make sure that the file has been copied over safely and then erase it from the hard disk. Then either write the contents of the floppy disk on its label, or give the disk a number and then against that number write the contents in a note book.

Obviously always take great care when deleting a file as mistakes can be difficult to rectify. It **is** possible to recover a deleted file but you will need a special recovery program to do it. This may already exist on your computer's system. Consult the manual or a computer literate friend. If you don't have a recovery program then switch off the computer. **Do not use it** again until you have the software. If you do save any document on to the disk then it is likely to overwrite your deleted document and that will be that.

CASE STUDIES

Jane

Jane has by now started using the word processor, not just for her college work, but also to write letters to friends and to write job applications. So she decides upon a directory structure like this: COLLEGE, PERSONAL and JOB.

She has created sub-directories in each of these. For College she has created: English, Geog(raphy), Econ(omics) and Business as these are the subjects she is taking. Several of the courses she further divides into other sub-directories so she now has sub-directories within sub-directories. She could go on doing this indefinitely. Jane has created this tidy directory structure because of the mistakes she made early on by not really caring where her documents were located on the hard disk. Eventually her documents had so many similar names that she didn't know what was what, which meant she had to keep on retrieving a document, opening it to find what it was all about, and then having to close and open up another if it was the wrong one.

Pam

Pam knows the importance of saving her work, but found it hard to get into the habit, especially when she was engrossed in an essay or letter. Finally, she started using a little timer that rang a bell every 25 minutes.

She also learned another lesson: not to use a complicated or powerful command before saving her document. This was brought home to her when she used a command called Search and Replace to change the word man for woman. But Pam set the command up wrongly, forgetting that the letters 'man' appear in lots of other words such as management, Manchester and command. Her word processor did what she asked with the result that 'man' was replaced anywhere the word processor found it. It took Pam a very long time to sort out the document. Now if she had only saved the document before performing the command, she could just have exited without saving the changed document and retrieved the original.

Alex

Now that he has started word processing Alex is surprised just how many different documents he is writing to different people every day. Of course, he has created what he thinks is a more than adequate directory structure, but it is pretty tedious switching between directories to save client letters and reports, especially when he finds that he is sometimes in and out of particular client directories four or five times every day. So, for convenience and to save himself as much time as possible, through the day he saves all of the documents that he creates and works on in a temporary directory, called CURRENT. At the end of the day he distributes all these files into their correct directories. This means that he can often transfer four or five documents into a directory at one go.

The only danger of this system is if Alex does not do this distribution process at the end of every day and documents start being 'stored' in this directory. If you set up such a current directory then you must keep it solely for documents that are currently being worked on.

Michael

For his writing business, Michael sets up a very simple directory structure on his computer. He sets up five main directories: ARTICLES, STORIES, QUERIES, PROPOSALS and INVOICES, but doesn't bother to create any sub-directories, just saving all of his documents under each appropriate heading. This is very straightforward at first, but Michael finds that when he has 30 or so files in any one directory it is more efficient to set up sub-directories, rather than look through 40 or 50 names trying to find the document he wants.

7
Printing Out Your Work

GETTING READY TO PRINT

Having written and edited your text you will at some stage want to print it out. However, you will first need to ensure that your printer understands what the computer and word processor are telling it to do.

To do this you need to **install** your printer. Your word processing manual will tell you how to do this. Very often it is just a matter of telling your word processor what make of printer you are using and the word processor will install it automatically.

Putting paper in your printer

How you put paper into your printer depends on what type of printer it is. If you have a dot matrix or daisywheel printer then it has a platen. This looks like a rolling pin and the paper is fed around it. When the platen rotates, the paper is moved upward. The paper should be inserted upside down and with the side you want to print on facing away from you so that when the paper goes under the platen and comes up the other side it will be the right way up and with the right side showing.

Until you are comfortable with this, make a note to yourself and stick it on the printer. With printers that have platens, you can make a copy of what you are printing by putting a carbon paper beneath the top sheet.

With other types of printer, such as laser and ink-jet, you don't have to feed in sheets of paper because the printer picks them up automatically from an internal tray.

To start printing you will need to activate the word processor's **Print** command. How this is done will vary between word processors. Follow your manual for guidance. There is always one thing to remember before printing, **always save your document**. For the most part there won't be a problem when printing out, but it is another variable that can throw a spanner in the works.

Printing on letterheads

When you print on plain paper you can start and finish printing on it wherever you want. However, when you use letterheads you will have to make allowance for any logos and company information that's at the top of the page. To do this, measure the distance from the top of the sheet to the point where you want your letter to begin. This distance will then be your top margin. Be generous in your calculations and try not to cramp your text right up to the bottom of the letterhead, logo or address (see Fig. 9). You can either make this the default setting or just change the setting of each document when you print on letterheads.

However, if you do this and you are printing a document of more than one page you will have a large space at the top of the second page, which doesn't have a letterhead. You *can* overcome this by printing the first page and then changing the top margin setting on your word processor for subsequent pages.

With dot matrix and daisywheel printers, which have a platen, this is not so much of a problem. All you need to do is insert the paper into the printer so that the printerhead of the printer is where you want the first line of text. Set the word processor's top margin setting to 0 and start printing. You can do this for all subsequent pages if you want.

Printing on more than one page

Your word processor can automatically number the pages you print out. You can dictate where you want the number to appear (left, right, or centre, top or bottom). These page numbers won't appear on screen.

If you intend to use page numbering then avoid the mistake of typing in the page numbers yourself. If you do then you will have to alter each page number if you add or remove a page. Worse still, if you add or remove text, you will alter the length of the page which means that you can end up with your page numbers half way up a page, which is not at all where you want them. So, leave page numbering to your word processor.

SETTING THE LENGTH OF A PAGE

When you have typed so many lines of your document, your word processor will automatically move onto a new page. It will show you that it has done this by putting a horizontal line right across the screen dividing one page from another. Something like this:

The location information shown on the status line at the bottom of the

Fig. 9. When printing on letterheads make the distance A-B your top margin.

screen will also show that you have moved onto a new page. Where the word processor begins this new page depends on the setting you have given for page length in the word processor's settings. When the word processor divides up a page like this it puts in a **page break**.

Ending a page

You don't have to wait until your word processor automatically inserts a page break: you can insert your own whenever you want. For instance, you might want to do this if the word processor would put its automatic page break in an inconvenient place, perhaps placing the bulk of a paragraph on one page and just one line or word on the next.

The page breaks that your word processor inserts are called **soft page breaks**. The page breaks that you insert are known as **hard page breaks**. Soft page breaks will always occur after a set number of lines, so even if you add or erase lines they will always be in the same position. Hard page breaks on the other hand move up and down the page as you add or erase lines above them.

Counting lines

There may be times when you will want to find out how many lines there are on a page, perhaps if you are trying to fit your words into a particular space. Every word processor is fitted with a status line that tells you which page and line you are on. So you can work out the number of lines of text you've typed by placing the cursor on the first line of the text you're measuring, noting the number, then using PgDn to move down the document, counting how many empty lines there are (for example between paragraphs) until you reach the last line of text you want to measure. Note the number of this and then subtract the first number you noted away from it. This difference is the number of text lines in a block. A more longwinded way to count the number of lines in a block is to simply move the cursor key down one line at a time, counting the number of times you hit the key.

CHECKLIST

Some word processors let you look at the complete layout of your document before you print it out, so you can check that paragraphs are in the right place and that margins are sufficient. However, spending a few moments checking over a document before you print it out is better than finding that you have made a major mistake when you have printed out all the document, especially if you are using expensive company letterheads or stationery. The following checklist should help you.

1. Have you checked the document for spelling?

2. Is the page set to the right length?

3. Are the margins on the document properly set?

4. Do you want page numbering on?

5. Are you numbering from the right page?

6. Are you printing in the right typeface in the right type size?

7. Are you using the right sort of paper?

8. Have you asked for the right number of copies?

WHEN YOUR PRINTER DOESN'T WORK

There are a number of reasons why your printer might not work, most of them relatively simple to correct.

- Make sure that your printer is **turned on** and all the leads that should be are connected correctly.

- Check that the printer is **properly installed** so that it knows what the word processor is talking about.

- Check whether the computer is **online**, that is ready to receive instructions from your printer. A light on the front or top of your printer will generally tell you when it is ready for action.

- Has the printer run out of **ribbon** or **toner**? You should always keep sufficient printer supplies, such as ribbons, toner, daisywheels and ink cartridges, to hand and have more than you need. If you don't then you can guarantee that just when you have an urgent piece of work to complete, you will run out of supplies and find that the only cartridge/toner/ribbon you do have is faulty!

If the printer doesn't print then just don't keep on trying to print. Your computer may still be sending the document to the printer. Issuing another printer command will probably just result in you having two copies of the document.

If you stop a printing job midway through, then be careful when you print out the next job. You might find that you end up printing the back end of the previous job, instead of the one you want. To avoid this you will have to go into the print settings and cancel the previous print job. Your word processor's manual will tell you how to do this.

If during printing the paper becomes jammed then stop printing immediately by hitting the Pause button on the printer. Turn the printer off and open it up. Remove the paper carefully, making sure that no scraps are left lying around or jammed anywhere.

CASE STUDIES

Jane

Jane is concerned that she's wasting too much paper when she prints out her documents, though she knows that even the most experienced word processor users rarely get all their printing right first time. It's not just that paper is expensive, she is also a member of Friends of the Earth and doesn't like to think of trees being destroyed just so that she can throw paper in the bin. She therefore begins recycling her paper. When she prints out a draft of documents so that she can proofread them, she uses the backs of old essays, or the blank side of junk mail that she's received. She does the same when she prints out the final draft of her essays, because she knows that no matter how carefully she proofreads the document on screen she will find a glaring spelling mistake as soon as she prints out. She is careful, however, to keep suitable scrap paper flat and to remove staples and paperclips – she knows how frustrating a paper jam can be!

Alex

After some weeks of writing and printing out letters to clients one by one, Alex thinks that he can increase his productivity and efficiency. Instead of printing out documents as he finishes them, he saves in a single file that he calls PRINTOUT. Then, an hour or so before the evening post he retrieves this file onto his screen and then prints out everything in one go, one letter after another. Alex estimates that if he has 20 or 30 letters to write in a day this can save him somewhere between 40 and 50 minutes because the word processor and printer don't have to gear themselves up for 30 different files. The only real disadvantage that Alex finds with this 'batch printing' is that he has to keep quite a careful eye on the printing, since errors can creep in. If a mistake happens at the beginning of the batch then he could waste an awful lot of paper.

There is another way that Alex could have batch printed. Instead of retrieving the document to the screen he could print straight from disk without having to call up the document on screen at all. This saves even more time, but you must be sure that you don't want to alter the file in any way. An option in your word processor's print settings will show you how to 'print out from disk'.

Pam

Pam is doing part-time word processing work for a company of estate agents. This involves her in printing out on all manner of materials, not just the company's letterheads, but also plain sheets of paper, property detail sheets, envelopes and labels. She even has to do a monthly report printed out on continuous or fanfold paper, which consists of many sheets of paper joined together at their perforated top and bottom edges. All this was a little confusing at first and Pam dreads to think of the amount of materials that she wasted, but she quickly got the hang of things. Fortunately for Pam her word processor allows her to set different print formats for different types of paper.

Michael

Michael has just finished writing his latest book and is ready to print it out. To prevent pages getting lost, it's standard practice for an author to type a shortened version of the book title and the author's name at the top of every page of the manuscript, and also a page number at the bottom of every page. This would be a tedious procedure with a typewriter. Think of doing this for a 500 page manuscript! You would have to write probably another 2500-3000 words just putting in the headers and then you would have to keep track of the page number each time. With word processing this is no problem. Michael just calls up his print option menu and tells it to print the title of his book at the top of the page on the left, and his surname on the right, both underlined. He also tells the computer to insert a couple of empty lines beneath this information at the top of the page, which is known as the 'header', and the printer will automatically insert it like this:

The Enchanted Archipelago *Jonson*

The page numbers are automatically inserted at the bottom of every page. Michael could have asked the printer to automatically print a 'footer', which is just like a header but at the bottom of every page. Headers or footers can just be one line, as in this case, or several.

Michael has one other working technique that's worth knowing. Because he has become somewhat paranoid about losing his written work, Michael makes a hard copy of each of the documents that he is working on, which means he has built up quite a library of copies of scripts, articles and manuscripts. To make sure that he knows where these scripts are stored on his computer, he writes on the front page of each script the directory and file name of that document. If he has made a copy of that file onto floppy he also writes the number of that floppy disk. And just to complete his thorough organisation he keeps a notebook in which he lists the contents of each floppy on separate pages.

8
Making Your Work Look Better

With traditional typewriting it is very difficult to alter the way a document looks. Generally you can have only one typeface and the layout of a page can be altered only after considerable effort. Not so with the word processor which can let you put text on the page anywhere and in any way you want to quickly and easily.

CHANGING THE WIDTH OF THE PAGE

At any one time your computer's screen will probably let you see as many as 80 characters in a row of text. But because a line of 80 characters won't fit on a standard width of paper, and because a line of this length is also more difficult to read, you can reduce the 'width' of the screen by setting **margins**. The margins you set will determine whether your text will fit on a sheet of paper when you print it out.

The wider the margins the less 'white' space you will have to write on in the middle. The narrower the margins the more writing area you will have. You can't write in the margins themselves. You can also have margins at the top and bottom of the page.

Your word processor will have default settings for margins. These are very often set at one inch for the left and right margins. You can alter these either for single pages or for all of the document. If you want to change the margins for all your future documents then you need to alter the word processor's default settings.

After you've made alterations to a document, such as changing the margins, your word processor will automatically move the text around so that it fits the new measurements. This is known as **reformatting** and your word processor will do it whenever you add or remove text, or alter the way that it is laid out. This is what happens when this paragraph reformats itself to cope with wider margins.

After you've made alterations to a document, such as changing the margins, your word processor will automatically move the text around so that it fits into the new measurements. This is known as reformatting and your word processor will do it whenever you add or remove text, or alter the way that it is laid out. This is what happens when this paragraph reformats itself to cope with wider margins.

CHANGING LINES OF TEXT

If you look at a page of text – it doesn't matter whether it is a letter, a book, a brochure or a magazine – you will see that almost invariably each line of text starts up against the left hand margin, but will not always finish right up against the right hand margin of the page. Most lines of text in books, for instance, finish right against the right hand margin, but a line of text in a brochure is likely to fall short of the right hand side.

Where a line of text finishes in relation to the page margins is known as **justification**. There are several types of justification, all of which a word processor can do quickly and easily. These are:

Full justification
Each line of text starts at the left margin and ends at the right margin. If there are insufficient characters in the line to reach the right hand margin, the word processor will automatically put in spaces to ensure that it does – which can make text look very 'loose'. Full justification is very difficult to achieve using a typewriter. Your word processor will probably have a default setting that means it prints out using full justification. This paragraph is fully justified.

Left justification
Each line of text starts at the left margin, but will only end at the right margin if there are exactly enough characters to fill up the line completely. If there aren't enough to do this the line will stop short of the right margin and the cursor will automatically go on to the line below. Only one space is left between words so left justified text has a charac-

teristic ragged look at its right hand edge with different lengths of text lines making up the document. For this reason it is also known as 'ragged right' (and you will sometimes see it referred to as 'ranged left'.) This type of justification looks more natural and is easier to read than fully justified text, especially if you are writing personal letters. This paragraph is left justified.

Right justification

This is the reverse of left justified text as each line of text starts at the right margin and finishes short of the left. The document has a ragged look at its left edge. If you use right justified text, you do not need to worry about where to start the line, the word processor will decide this for you automatically. You will use right justified (or 'ranged right') text very rarely, if at all. This paragraph is right justified.

Centre justification

The start and end of each line of text is an equal distance from the left and right hand edges of the text. It is literally 'centred' between the margins. You would use centred text to print out such things as menus or to put headings mid-way between margins. Using an ordinary type-writer to do this is difficult and time consuming. This paragraph is centre justified.

GETTING RID OF TEXT

You've already seen how using the Delete and Backspace keys can erase unwanted text. This is fine if you only want to erase a single character or just a few words, but what if you want to erase several paragraphs or even several pages of text? Using the Delete and Back-space keys would be very time consuming indeed. A far quicker way is to use what are known as **block commands** and though different word processors do this in different ways, the principle is the same.

First, you have to mark the block of text you want to erase. To do this, position the cursor at the start of the text block and 'anchor' it, perhaps by using the Enter key, or a combination of keys (your word processor's manual will tell you what to do). Then using the cursor keys or PgDn or PgUp keys, move to the end of the block you want to erase. As the cursor moves you will see that it pulls a 'highlight' bar behind it. With colour monitors this bar will be in a different colour from the main screen. With black and white monitors it will appear as a brighter bar.

Note that if you want to erase several lines you don't need to move

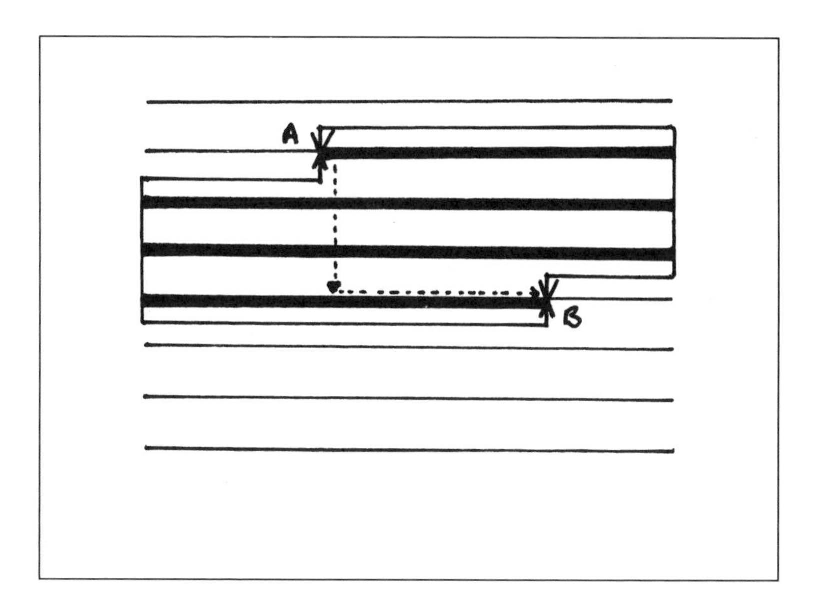

Fig. 10. Marking a block of text with the cursor. (To mark the block A-B you do not need to send the cursor all along each line of text. You can use the down cursor key to move to the right line of text and then the cursor right key to move to the appropriate place on the line.)

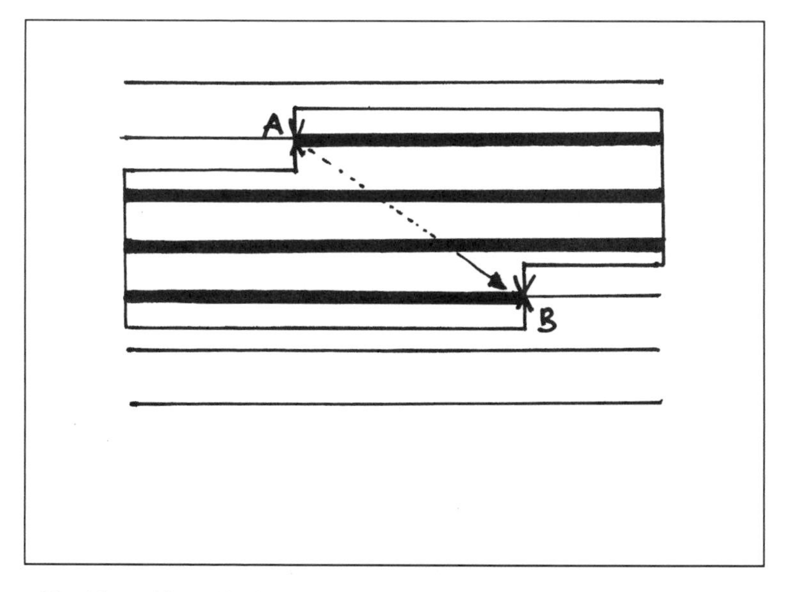

Fig. 11. marking a block of text with a mouse. (To mark the block A-B when using a mouse you need only drag the cursor straight from A to B.)

the cursor along each line; just use the up and down cursor keys to take the cursor to the next line and all text to the right of the cursor will be automatically highlighted (see Figs. 10 and 11).

Having reached the end of the block you want to erase you will need to anchor that end of it using the appropriate key; again consult your word processor manual. Having now marked the block, you can use the Delete command to erase it. When you activate Delete you may be asked 'Do you wish to erase block Y/N?' Press the 'Y' key and the block will be erased. Some word processors may require you to reverse the process by telling them first that you want to Delete before marking the block.

The Delete command is a useful one because it allows you to remove sections of your text quickly and very easily.

Any text below the block you have erased will automatically move up to fill the space that the erased text used to occupy. The word processor does this automatically for you.

Such text block operations are also known as **cut and paste**, that is cutting a block from one place and pasting it in another. And as well as using them to erase text, you can also use these commands to move and copy text to other places in a document, or even into another document.

Returning text to the screen

Even experienced word processor users make mistakes from time to time. And one of the worst is erasing text from a document when you don't mean to do it. This can cause a heart attack. However, whenever you delete text it is not lost forever immediately, but is rather tucked away temporarily, out of sight but not yet consigned to the waste paper basket.

This is a great help because if your word processor has an **undelete** command you can return your text to the screen. There is one problem, however. When a block of text is erased it is only stored temporarily in the computer's memory. If you have marked and deleted another block of text since, then it is the second block that you will undelete and not the first. Some word processors will, however, let you recall not only the last block of text that was deleted, but also the one before that, so all may not be lost.

Undelete is not only a highly useful command if you accidentally erase text or immediately change your mind once you have done it, but it has another use. You can use the Delete and Undelete commands as a quick way to move text around a document. To do this, mark and erase text using Delete, then move the cursor to the position you want to move the text to and activate the Undelete command and the text will reappear in its new position.

PUTTING DOCUMENTS TOGETHER

Sometimes you will want to move or copy a whole document into another one – for example, if one document has a lot of useful bits of information that you want to use elsewhere. Your word processor allows you to do this in one of two ways. You can either be in Document B and insert or 'read' document A into it or you can be in Document A and send or 'write' it into document B. (You can also write or read just a section of a document.) Once you have combined the documents you can delete the text that you don't want.

Creating a standard document

Though much word processing will involve producing individual letters, reports and proposals, there are many occasions when you will be creating a document that is only marginally different from many others. Invoices, statements, memos, faxsheet headers and reminders are all examples. How useful and time saving it would be to have a standard format of document into which you could simply insert new information. It is possible to do this by having special **template** documents. And though there is nothing really special about them, many people never think about using them. They are no more than documents that you have created before and which can act as a framework for similar documents – rather like blank forms just waiting for you to fill them in.

Action Point

Think of five template documents that you could create for your business, personal correspondence or leisure activities.

1. . . . .
2. . . . .
3. . . . .
4. . . . .
5. . . . .

SAVE YOUR TIME EDITING

Just as templates offer a highly effective means of creating a document quickly, so do **macros**. These are commands which allow you to automate certain tasks which you carry out regularly. For example, if you frequently put your name and address into a document, rather than having to key it in each time, you can create a macro for it. Then just by the press of a single key your name and address will appear magically at the cursor. A macro can either be specific to one particular document or usable in every document that you create. You could create macros for such things as signature blocks, for example:

Yours sincerely

Ian Phillipson
(Managing Director)

which you could enter into any document by just pressing the designated key.

Macros are invaluable if you have to make a lot of revisions to a text, since it is during this editing that you are at greatest risk from RSI. Unlike the time you spend writing your first draft when your fingers are moving many different keys and you can develop a good rhythm, editing means concentration, sometimes tension, and endlessly repeated movements of the cursor.

Though there are macro software packages commercially available, for the most part you will have to devise your own. The best way to do this is to start off with a particular word processing problem and solve it by creating a piece of sample text. When you have done this to your satisfaction then you can turn on the macro-making command and define the macro.

Macro checklist

Macros are very useful time savers. List five macros which would help you produce documents faster.

1. . . . .

2. . . . .

3. . . . .

4. . . . .

5. . . . .

SEARCHING FOR TEXT

The longer your document the longer it will take you to find a particular point in it, such as a word or name. However, the word processor knows a quick way of doing that using its **Search** command. This will look for any word you tell it to: in fact it doesn't have to be a proper word, but just a string of letters or even numbers. Most word processors will let you look both backwards and forwards. If the string of characters you are looking for is in the document they will stop when they reach it. If the string isn't there then your word processor will tell you.

While on the subject of searching this is a good time to bring up the concept of 'wild cards'. Wild cards are the chameleons of the word processing world because they can pretend to be any symbol. For instance, if you were looking through a document for the name of Mr Krycheck, but couldn't remember whether he spelt his name Kricheck, you could use a wild card character to stand for both the 'y' and 'i'. You would type Kr?check, where ? is the wild card character.

The Search command can come in very useful in finding where you finished working on a document, by inserting a bookmark, just as Michael does in the case study below.

Replacing a word

Search and Replace is a command similar to Search, but instead of just looking for a word or string of characters, this command finds a word then replaces it with another one. This can be particularly useful in a long document, for instance in a novel when you suddenly have a whim to change the name of your lead character.

CASE STUDIES

Jane

A couple of late nights with friends and a party or two have put Jane in a panic as she has to have a 10 page essay in for the next morning. She knows that what she has written is good, the trouble is that she only has eight pages and just can't think of anything else to write. Then Jane has a brainwave. Using the word processor's page format command she just widens the margins of the document by half an inch or so on each side and also increases them at the top and bottom of the page just for luck. Now when she reformats the document she finds that it fits onto ten pages. With that piece of creative thinking the problem was solved. (However, Jane's tutor closed that loophole when the next essay was set — he asked for a certain number of words rather than pages.)

Alex

At his accountancy practice, Alex is sending out his latest bunch of invoices. Before he discovered templates Alex used to word process each invoice individually, but very soon he began thinking that it was very stupid keying information that was virtually the same from invoice to invoice. So to save time he created an invoice template by retrieving a standard invoice that he has previously sent out to a client.

Much of the information is common to every invoice that Alex sends out: for instance, INVOICE and Invoice No: at the top of the page, Alex's address, and words such as TO:, FOR, Total and With Thanks. So Alex deletes the rest of the information that is specific only to that client and ends up with a template.

When he has done this, Alex saves the document under a suitable name such as TEMP-INV. Now the next time he has to send out an invoice, he simply calls up the file TEMP-INV and makes suitable alterations to it. The only thing that Alex must remember not to do is unthinkingly save the file under the name of TEMP-INV, otherwise the next time he retrieves it, it won't be a template document at all but a completed invoice. He would then have to go through the process again.

Pam

Like Alex, Pam is into template documents and not just invoices, but also memos, property details, monthly reports and letters. She goes about creating them in much the same way as Alex, but for greater convenience she has set up a whole directory of templates, called TEMPLATE. This means that she can simply go into the template directory and retrieve one of the files there, such as LETTER, DETAILS, REPORT, or MEMO and know that it will be a template.

Michael

Michael too has begun using templates to speed up his word processing, but he is also using macros in a big way, and has built up quite a library of them. When Michael wants to send out a letter, rather than create a template document for it, he has created a macro instead which puts 'Yours sincerely' and his signature properly laid out at the bottom of the page, just with a press of a key. He has also created a macro that puts a simple logo into a document.

One of the most useful macros that Michael has created is one that he uses when editing long lengths of text, such as book chapters. When he finishes work for the day Michael inserts a 'bookmark', a couple of unusual characters into the text, ** in Michael's case. Now when he sits down to work the next day, Michael activates that macro and the word processor automatically hunts for **, the place where Michael finished work the day before.

Michael has also been using the ability of his word processor to divide the monitor screen into segments such as halves and quarters, known as **windows**. (These should not be confused with Windows software.) Michael can have different documents in each window and can work on each in turn if he wants. Individual windows can be expanded so that they fill the entire monitor screen to give you a better view (see Fig. 12). This is very useful for Michael because he can copy or move sections of one document to another quickly and easily. Without this 'windowing' facility Michael would have to call one document on to screen, mark the block he wanted to copy or move, exit the document and call up the new one he wanted to put the block in, if his word processor would let him. Not all will allow you to transfer blocks of text between documents. So when you are buying new word processing software, check that it can create windows.

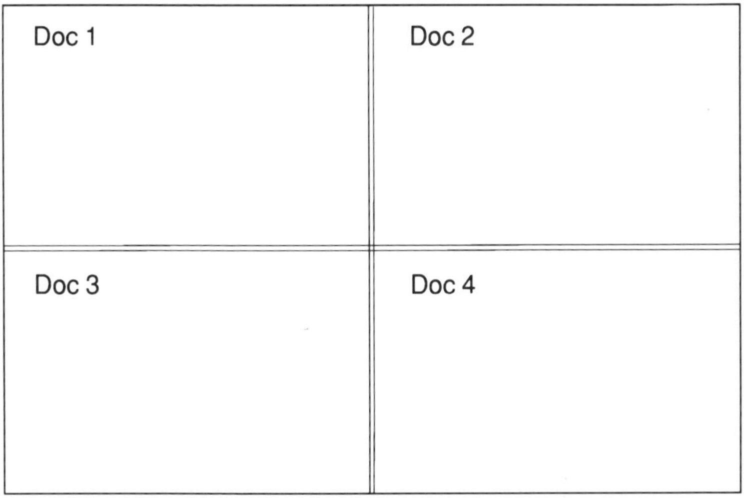

Doc 1	Doc 2
Doc 3	Doc 4

Fig. 12. A windowed screen.
(If your word processor has a split screen facility you can divide your word processor screen into windows, each of which can contain a different document. Small windows can be expanded so that they fill the monitor screen.)

9
Checking Your Work

Whenever you send out a letter, application, report or manuscript, no matter how long or short it is, people will notice if things are wrong. Like it or not, people will pick up your errors in spelling and grammar. Some might pass these off as just 'mistakes', but others will simply think you are slovenly, ill-educated or poorly qualified.

CHECKING YOUR SPELLING

Though some of the cheapest word processors don't have a spellchecking facility, most do. These work by comparing every word they find in a document with the words found in their own in-built dictionary. If the spellchecker finds a word that it doesn't recognise, it will stop at the word and give you the option of replacing it with a suggested word or editing it. The spellchecker will also allow you to add new words into the dictionary to cater for your own specialised needs. In this way your spellchecker can be 'taught' to recognise certain words by looking through one dictionary rather than another. (See Michael's way of working in Case Study 2 below.)

Another type of tool that you can use with your spellchecker is a thesaurus. This will provide you with a list of synonyms, words that mean the same - or almost the same - as the word you want.

Dangers of the spellchecker

You should be careful about immediately adding every word your spellchecker doesn't recognise in its dictionary. If you do, then it's possible that the spellchecker might then pass over a word used out of context as being right. For instance, if you add every plural that you come across, how would your spellchecker ever warn you that there was something wrong?

CHECKING YOUR GRAMMAR

Grammar checkers work by picking up on different types of grammatical errors in your document, such as capital letters in the wrong place, incorrect punctuation, agreement of verb and subject and inappropriate adjective use. Grammar checkers will even advise you on style points. They can be useful in highlighting the fact that you use a certain word too many times, or if you are writing long sentences too frequently.

CHECKING YOUR HYPHENATION

Hyphenation is a way of splitting up words that are too long to fit on a line. When used in the writing of fully justified text, hyphenation can make your work look more attractive to the reader's eye.

You can set your word processor to hyphenate for you and it will put a hyphen in a place of its choosing and reformat the text accordingly. If you make changes to the text so that the word now fits on a line, the word processor will automatically remove the hyphen and reformat the text so that the word is joined up.

The hyphen that the word processor uses during hyphenation is not the same hyphen found on the keyboard. Hyphens made with the keyboard do not disappear if the text is reformatted and you would be left with an unnecessary hyphen in the middle of a word.

If you do use automatic hyphenation, don't always expect to agree with your word processor's choice of position for the hyphen. Ultimately be guided by your own eye because incorrectly divided words make text harder to read.

How to hyphenate

These are some rules of hyphenation that you might like to use to check whether your word processor's hyphenation command is dividing words appropriately.

Divide words

- only when you have to
- between syllables (num-ber, know-ledge)
- between double letters (quar-rel, com-mittee) unless the double letter comes at the end of a simpler form of the word (call-ing, success-ful, add-ing)

- only where the hyphen already exists in hyphenated words (forty-five and not for-ty-five)

- at a prefix or suffix, but not within a prefix or suffix (super-market and not su-permarket, contra-ceptive and not con-traceptive)

- so the most meaningful group of letters is created (careless-ness and not care-lessness, consign-ment and not con-signment)

- after, and not before a one-letter syllable (busi-ness, deli-cate, sili-con) unless that one-letter syllable is part of the suffix *-able* or *-ible* (illeg-ible, move-able, inevit-able, permiss-ible)

- words with three or more consonants together in the place that the word's pronunciation suggests (watch-ing and not wat-ching, chil-dren and not child-ren).

Don't divide:

- words which only have one syllable

- words which have fewer than six letters

- one-letter syllables (alone and not a-lone)

- two-letter syllables at the end of a word (caller and not call-er)

- before the suffixes (-ical, -icon, -cious, -tious, -tial, -sion, -ceous, -geious, -sial, -tion, -gion, -gious)

- abbreviations, contractions or someone's name

- the last word of a paragraph or the last word of a page.

PROOFREADING YOUR WORK

Because words are so easily produced and altered using the word processor it is easy to be slapdash about checking your work as thoroughly as you might. And no matter how many word processing tools you use to check your work, such as spellcheckers and grammar checkers, the final decision must rest with your own eyes and judgement. So, to ensure that all is correct you must proofread every document carefully and thoroughly. These guidelines should help you do that.

- Especially when you are typing quickly it is easy to turn around the position of letters in a word, just like htis (this). Look carefully at words to see if you have put the characters in the right order.

- Check to see that you haven't inserted an extra letter in a word because you haven't hit a key cleanly and have pressed more than one at a time, just like thgis.

- Check that no characters have been left out of words, just like ths. These errors are particularly difficult to spot if it is a vowel that's missing.

- Look out for a space omitted between words, such asthis.

- If you have used brackets (parentheses) make sure that the characters within them come right up against them, like (this) and not like (this).

- Have you left a double space at the end of a full stop? Like this. Double spaces are the norm when typing, but for word processing it is usual just to leave one space only.

- Have you closed up all sets of ''quote marks''or have you left one set ''off, like this?

- Are all the headings consistent in a document. Or are some HEADINGS in upper case and others a mixture of Lower and Upper Case?

- Have you been consistent in the number of lines of space you put between paragraphs? It doesn't matter whether you change the spacing for different documents, just so long as you are consistent within a document.

- Make sure that page breaks are in the right place so that there are no widows and orphans. A widow is the first line of a paragraph printed as the last line on a page. An orphan is the last line of a paragraph printed as the first line of a new page (see Fig. 13).

TOP OF PAGE

sadly for her mother and father.

The above is an example of an orphan, that is the last line of a paragraph printed as the first line of a new page. Orphans are considered bad because they look ugly.

Below is an example of a widow, that is the first line of a paragraph is printed as the last line of a page. The rest of the paragraph is on the next page. Widows are considered bad because they look ugly.

Widows in printed document are nothing to do

BOTTOM OF PAGE

Fig. 13. An example of a widow and an orphan.

- If you have moved text around and then deleted some of it, make sure that you haven't left any of the text lying around: punctuation marks are particularly easy to overlook.

- Have you left spaces before a punctuation mark so that it hangs in mid air , like this?

- Have you repeated a word in a sentence, like this this?

- Have you held the Shift key down a little too long when capitalizing so that the second letter is capitalised? LIke this.

The above is not an exhaustive set of proofreading rules, but they do cover many of the commonest errors that you can make. You can set up macros that will do many of these tasks for you. Consult your manual on how to define a macro.

Action point

Practise proofreading by casting your eye down any piece of text you come across, not just your own documents. Word process a section of this chapter quickly (all of it if you wish), then proofread it for accuracy.

Learn how to use proofmarks. These are a special set of marks that editors use to indicate errors in scripts and copy.

CASE STUDIES

Jane

Jane is looking for a job and is sending applications out left, right and centre. But her high level of activity and enthusiasm is causing problems when she writes covering letters. Pushed for time, Jane 'recycles' an old covering letter, sending it out with just a change of address at the top of the page. But when she wrote that first letter, Jane missed an error: 'now' instead of 'know' in the very first paragraph of the letter. Of course, to her spellchecker that was fine. Confident that she had checked the letter, out it went. Is it any surprise that Jane's job hunting hasn't been too successful? Even if you are using a form letter, proofread it from time to time as errors can creep in.

Michael

In his wide ranging writing, which includes articles on technical subjects, such as computers, as well as general articles, Michael has encountered a problem when spellchecking his words. For example, when he is writing about computers he often wants to use the expression 'electronic mail'. His spellchecker's dictionary recognises this without any problem. However, electronic mail is generally shortened in computer-speak to 'e-mail' which the spellchecker identifies as a misspelled word.

After it has done this a few times, Michael is all set to add the word to his dictionary, but then he has a thought. Of course he wants the spellchecker to recognise e-mail in his computer articles, but not in his more general writing where e-mail is more likely to be a spelling error. If he adds the word to his main dictionary the spellchecker would just let it through. So Michael creates a special 'computer' dictionary that is the only one to recognise e-mail. Michael loads this 'supplementary' dictionary before he checks technical documents and the problem is solved. Creating supplementary dictionaries is one of the best ways of keeping control of your spellchecker so that it doesn't let every word through.

10
Personalising Your Mailshots

DOING A SIMPLE MAILSHOT

One of the most tedious tasks any business or organisation can undertake is the mailshot, that's sending out the same information to many different people on a mailing list.

At its simplest this involves printing names and addresses on envelopes or labels. Using conventional typing to do such a task is not only time-consuming but wasteful - after doing one mailshot, you have to type out the names and addresses all over again when you want to do another one. As you have seen, the ability of the word processor to store information means that when names and addresses have been keyed in once they can be used over and over again.

PERSONALISING YOUR MAILSHOT

At a more complicated level, the word processor allows you to create a standard document and then put variable items of information, such as names, addresses and telephone numbers, where you want them in the document. This is a very useful facility to have because it lets you produce personalised sales letters, statements and reports to prospective clients, suppliers or members of clubs. Personalised mailshots are doubly useful if you already have that personal information on computer.

When you ask your word processor to do this it is called 'mail merging'. There are two stages to mail merging:

- First, you have to create the letter you want sent out to everybody. This is like any standard letter but you will leave spaces in it where you want the word processor to put personalised information, such as names, addresses and telephone numbers. When you create a letter like this it is known as the primary file.

- Secondly, you have to tell the word processor where you want the personalised information to go.

Case study: Pam

This is the letter that Pam created for one of the sales negotiators while working at the estate agency.

. . . .
. . . .
. . . .
. . . .
. . . .
. . . .

Dear . . . .

Enclosed are some property details which I hope you will find interesting and suitable.

If you need any further help . . . . or would like to arrange a viewing of any of the properties, then please call me.

Yours sincerely

James Jameson

The dotted lines indicate where a space has been left for a name, an address or date. And so that her word processor knows that she doesn't want these spaces left as just spaces, Pam has to insert special codes in them. (Your word processor manual will tell you what special code you should put in the spaces.) When the special codes of word processor WordPerfect are inserted, Pam's document would look like this:

{FIELD} 1 {FIELD} 2
{FIELD} 3
{FIELD} 4
{FIELD} 5
{FIELD} 6 {FIELD} 7

{FIELD} 8

Dear {FIELD} 1 {FIELD} 2

Enclosed are some property details which I hope you will find interesting and suitable.

If you need any further help {FIELD}1 {FIELD}2 or would like to arrange a viewing of any of the properties, then please call me.

Yours sincerely

James Jameson

The term FIELD is really just a fancy name for one piece of information. In this case:

{FIELD} 1 means First Name
{FIELD} 2 means Surname
{FIELD} 3 means First line of the address
{FIELD} 4 means Second line of the address
{FIELD} 5 means Town
{FIELD} 6 means County
{FIELD} 7 means Post code
{FIELD} 8 means Date

The { } are used to tell the word processor that the FIELD is not just another word, but the special mail merge code. The word processor automatically puts in {FIELD}1, {FIELD}2, {FIELD}3 etc at the places where Pam wants to incorporate information. These expressions do not appear when the document is printed out. This is how Pam's document appears when printed out.

> Mrs Mayfield
> 123 Molehill Road
> Molehill Park
> Molehill-on-Thames
> London N1 2NP
>
> 17 September 199X
>
> Dear Mrs Mayfield
>
> Enclosed are some property details which I hope you will find interesting and suitable.
>
> If you need any further help Mrs Mayfield or would like to arrange a viewing of any of the properties, then please call me.
>
> Yours sincerely
>
> James Jameson

With the laser printer going at full speed, in this way Pam can send out hundreds and hundreds of letters very easily and quickly. This is just one instance of being able to re-use information (names and addresses) already held on computer disk.

Personalising even more

As you've already seen each of these pieces of information is known as a field and you can have as many of them as you want. Indeed, the more fields that you can break your information into the better, because it gives you a more flexible approach to your mailing. For example, if your Name Field contained only the whole of the name, you would have to start your letter 'Dear Eric Smith', or 'Dear Jane Jones'. However, if you had split the Name Field into two parts (a First Name and a Surname) then you could still print Eric Smith or Jane Jones on the envelope but start your letter in a more friendly way with just 'Dear Eric' or 'Dear Jane', while still addressing the envelope with the full name.

Your word processor should also allow you to suppress the printing out of certain fields if you don't want them to appear. Using this facility you could then include something like a client's telephone number in the record but only have it printing out on rare occasions. So, even if only a few of the people you are mailing to have a company name, you still need to include a company-name field.

These are the basic principles of mail merging, but every word processor has its own special way of working. Consult your manuals about how exactly you should go about setting up a primary and secondary file, and how you should enter fields.

Action point

Write down a list of fields that you might want to include in a mailing for your business, work or leisure.

. . . .

. . . .

. . . .

. . . .

. . . .

. . . .

. . . .

. . . .

CASE STUDIES

Jane

Term is over and Jane is now in the job market. As well as going through the local newspapers and magazines, Jane goes to the town's library and begins copying out the names and addresses of prospective employers from local and trade directories. She has managed to borrow a laptop so she can key the information direct into that, which saves much time because she doesn't have to spend hours writing notes, then trying to decipher her terrible handwriting and then finally keying the names and addresses into her computer.

Jane hasn't bothered to learn how to mail merge on her machine so when she gets home she just types the names and addresses onto the top of a standard letter rather than letting the word processor do this automatically and then prints out each one. She then deletes that address from the top of the letter and types in the next one, and so on. It's not the most sophisticated way of producing a direct mail letter, but it is perhaps the simplest way of sending out a lot of letters if you can't get to grips with mail merge.

Alex

Alex is moving his accountancy practice and has to notify his clients of his change of address and telephone number very quickly. He needs to send out a standard letter, but doesn't need it personalised, so all he does is set up his laser printer to print his client addresses onto adhesive address labels, which he has bought in sheets of A4 which fit into the printer's tray. Within minutes he has sheets of completed labels. These he just peels off and sticks onto envelopes. Simple and easy and all using information that he has already keyed into the computer.

11
Developing Your Word Processing

By now you should have a very clear idea of how word processing can help you write and produce written work of the very highest quality. But there is more, so this final chapter covers a couple of areas that aren't strictly word processing, but nevertheless really are blood brothers to it: outlining software and desktop publishing.

PLANNING YOUR WRITING

Before writing any document, whether it is a letter or a report, many people like to create a framework which they can then fill out. Traditionally these 'outlines' are written on a sheet of paper and are really no more than subject headings to be covered in the document. For shorter documents an outline is simple because there are only a few areas to be covered. And of course for very short documents, or informal ones you probably wouldn't bother with an outline at all. But for longer documents they are of great benefit because they help you plan not only exactly what you want to say, but also the order in which you are going to say it. Traditionally you would create an outline on a sheet of paper, scribbling down subject headings and particular points that you might want to make about a subject. Fig. 14. shows the written outline for Chapter 2 of this book.

But as with any work that involves committing words to paper, you can't easily make changes and if you want to move things around, well that's not easy either. So, to help in this planning process, a cut-down version of the word processor has been created, the outliner which helps you organise your thoughts before committing anything to paper.

This is very much like the traditional word processor, but it automatically allows you to create headings for different topics and to show the relationship between ideas.

CHOOSING EQUIPMENT

What you need to start

Computer - monitor screen
- System unit
- hardware - definition
Software - definition
- Windows

types - IBM & Apple - pros & cons

Disks - floppy and hard - characteristics

Choosing Computer - speed - processor - type
- hard disk size
- monitor

Printer - types - pros & cons

Where to buy - High St
Computer store
Mail order
Auctions
Secondhand
} pros & cons of each

Maintenance - keyboard
- screen
} cover at night - cleaning

- checking wiring
- turning off
- virus - antivirus

Fig. 14. A written outline for Chapter 2 of How to Start Word Processing.

1. **Types of transport**

1.1. Land vehicles

1.1.1. Cars

1.1.2. Buses and coaches

1.1.3. Bicycles

1.1.1.1 Historic cycles

1.1.1.2 Modern cycles

1.1.1.3 Racing cycles

1.2 Water vehicles

1.2.1 Cruisers

1.2.2. Warships

1.2.3 Merchant vessels

1.3 Air vehicles

For example, if you wanted to show the relationship between types of transport you might end up with an outline that looks like the one shown above.
Types of Transport is a 'heading' and indicates that this is a major area in the outline. This heading has three subheadings: Land, Water and Air Vehicles. These subheadings can be divided further into other subheadings, for example: Cars, Buses and Bicycles, which in turn can be divided even more. The numbers let you keep track of where you are in the outline. The first numbers show you what level of heading you are on and the last item which item at that level you are looking at.

Having created an outline like this, you can start making notes on each section and filling out the text.

And if at any one time you want to have an overall or highly detailed picture of the outline you can do it by hiding some levels of heading. For example you can 'hide' everything but the main headings, so these are all that you see.

Many word processors come with an outliner already incorporated so that when you have finished using the outliner you simply switch over to the word processor and begin work on your outline immediately.

CREATING HIGH QUALITY DOCUMENTS

Starting desktop publishing

With your word processing skills and knowledge as a starting point, you will have a sound foundation for moving into the world of desktop publishing or DTP. This is a very good way of producing high quality documents, whether very simple or highly complex.

You will be interested in desktop publishing if you want to produce attractive newsletters for hobby groups or clubs, professional looking brochures and catalogues, and even quality magazines.

THE ADVANTAGES OF DTP

Desktop publishing differs from word processing in a number of ways:

- You can combine your words with pictures to create brochures, advertisements and newsletters. (You can do this to an extent with some more top of the range word processing packages, but only at a very simple level.)

- You are able to create more professional and better looking documents using DTP because you can so easily and readily alter typefaces and position exactly where on the page your text and illustrations appear. This gives you tremendous control over how your finished document looks.

- You can prepare and produce typeset quality copy that can be worked on straightaway by the printer. Normally you would pass your copy and graphics to a printer or designer who would then have to typeset the text in the kind and size of typeface that you want, and position it and graphics in the right place on the page before printing. This is costly. With DTP you have already chosen and laid out the type and pictures on the page, which the printer can start printing from immediately. What is more you can supply your desktop published document on a disk direct to the printer so that no design work or keying in has to be done by the print company.

CHOOSING EQUIPMENT FOR DTP

Your existing equipment may be powerful enough for desktop publishing, but if you have bought simply with word processing in mind, the chances are that it won't be.

The computer

Central to desktop publishing is a fast and powerful computer. Word processing is a relatively simple occupation for a computer and one which doesn't tax its memory and powers too greatly. Not so DTP.

The task of storing not only words, but different typefaces, pictures and remembering where everything is, eats up a terrific amount of computer memory. Therefore your computer will have as large a memory as you can afford, the larger the better.

Also because every DTP document contains a lot of information it can take the computer quite a long time to go through a file. The slower your computer the longer it will take. Even if a slow computer can handle your DTP software you might be waiting 10, 15 or 20 minutes for your computer to perform a task, during which you can't work on the document. Therefore the minimum requirement should be a 486 machine.

The monitor

Your computer will also need to have a high resolution monitor for effective DTP work. If it doesn't have one then you won't be able to position blocks of text or illustrations accurately on the screen and therefore on the page. A computer dealer should be able to advise you on your equipment needs for DTP.

The software

Though you will generally create the words of a document on a word processor, you will need DTP software to manipulate it. Numerous DTP packages are available, ranging from the simple to highly complex, 'professional' systems. Desktop publishing packages are one of the more difficult types of software to learn, far more so than the word processor. You will have to commit yourself to spending time learning exactly what a DTP system can do, if you are to get the most out of it. Even if you are at heart someone who likes to learn on their own, this might be the time to attend a course on a particular desktop publishing package.

The mouse

You may not have needed one for your word processing, but you will for DTP since a mouse is continually used to move text around to precise points within a document.

The printer

There is no point creating a document that looks highly professional on the screen but then looks terrible on paper because it is printed out poorly. A high resolution laser printer will enable you to print very crisp images.

The scanner

This piece of equipment is an essential if you want to incorporate photographs and illustrations into your publications. A scanner works rather like a photocopier by 'scanning' over the illustration and converting what it sees into signals that the computer and DTP software can understand, manipulate and store. If you are not going to use illustrations in your DTP documents then you don't need a scanner. Alternatively you can just produce the text as you want it and then ask the printing company you are using to incorporate illustrations where you want them.

DO YOU NEED DTP?

Do you often have to create attractive documents that must look very good to impress clients and customers? Yes No

Using DTP you can create very high quality and professional looking documents.

Do you need to include graphics and illustrations in your written work? Yes No

Unlike word processing, DTP can easily handle and manipulate illustrations and graphics.

Do you spend a lot of money on typesetting? Yes No

DTP lets you produce work that is of typesetting standard and from which the printer can work. So you don't have to pay anyone else to do your typesetting.

Do you ask other people to design documents and then find they haven't done it as you want? Yes No

With DTP you can play around with the design until it is as *you* want it.

LEARNING TO DESIGN

Desktop publishing software offers an immense menu of design tools and if you are not careful you can end up trying to use all of them. Then you don't end up with a good design but a dog's dinner. Therefore try to learn as much as you can about document design before starting DTP, then master a few of the techniques before branching out. It is better to be good in just a few areas than average in many. There are numerous design courses on the subject.

CASE STUDIES

Pam

Pam has been asked to help out with a newsletter for the parents' association at her children's school. The newsletter isn't too exotic, but using her word processing skills and the school's DTP software she can produce a four page publication with two columns per page and a few graphics thrown in for good measure. At a pinch she could have done all of this on a reasonable word processor, but it was easier with DTP and besides Pam rather likes using the system. And once she has produced a few simple publications she will be looking to create better, more complicated newsletters which only DTP can do.

Michael

With things going so well for him, Michael has set up his own self-publishing company so he can control nearly all of the production of written materials - writing the words, combining them with illustrations, designing and laying out pages and then producing pages that are of sufficient quality that they are ready to go straight to the printer. The only thing he doesn't do himself is the actual printing. Michael does all this using a top of the range DTP system.

Glossary

ALT Key — the Alternative key, used in conjunction with other keys to issue commands.

ASCII — a universal language that allows one word processor to use documents that have been created on a different word processor. When a document has been converted into ASCII text it will lose all its special word processing characteristics, such as bold and underline.

Back up — saving files onto floppy disks or a hard drive, so that you have a copy of your work in the event of power or computer failure.

Block — a section of work within a document on which commands, such as move, copy and delete, can be performed.

Boilerplating — an individual document that is created by selecting sections of other documents.

Bold — characters on screen and during printing that are thicker and darker than other characters.

Booting up — turning the computer on.

Carriage return — needs to be performed at the end of a line of text to move down to the next line when typing. Carriage returns are not necessary in word processing.

Centred text text that appears equidistant between the left and right margins of a document.

Close down turning a computer off.

Codes characters which aren't printed out, but which instruct your computer and printer to perform a specific function, such as underlining text.

Continuous stationery sheets of paper attached to one another, but which can be separated by tearing the perforated line that separates them.

CPS characters per second. The rate at which a printer can print out.

CTRL key the Control key, used in conjunction with other keys to issue commands.

Cursor the flashing block that appears on the monitor screen and where characters are typed.

Cut and paste cutting text from one section of a document and moving it to another section of the same, or another, document.

Daisywheel printer a type of printer that uses a rotating disk of letters and numbers to make an imprint on the printer ribbon.

Default settings the setting for margins, line spacing and other printer and computer operations which are pre-set. Default settings can be changed.

Desktop publishing also known as DTP, this is a combination of hardware and software that allows you to produce high quality and well designed copy, artwork and publications.

Delete erasing text from a document. Also erasure of a file from a directory.

Directory an area of the computer in which similar files and documents are stored.

Document a word processing file. It can range from just a word to a letter to a book.

Dot matrix printer a printer that uses a pattern of small pins to make an imprint on the printer ribbon.

DOS the Disk Operating System. This contains the command programs that manage the computer's memory and files. It is rather like the engine of a car — your computer has to have it to go.

Editing the changes made to a document, such as erasing words and moving text.

Escape a key that allows you to cancel a word processing operation.

Exit a command sent to a word processing application to stop it working.

Fast keys also known as accelerator keys, these are key combinations that move you immediately to a particular part of the document you are working on: the top of the document, the bottom of the document, the next page, the previous page etc.

Field a variable item of information (such as name, or line of an address) that can be inserted into a standard document.

File a document that can be stored on disk and retrieved.

..k	a disk of magnetic material used for storing information.
Foo..r	a line, or a number of lines, which are added automatically at the bottom of every page of a document you print out. You set the number of lines between the header and the bottom of the page of text.
Format line	this displays on the monitor screen document margins and tab settings.
Function keys	special keys that allow you to issue commands to the word processor.
Global search and replace	searching for all occurrences of a word or string of characters in a document.
Go to	a command that allows you to go straight to a line, page or marker that you specify.
GUI	Graphical User Interface: an operating system for the computer in which you issue commands by pointing at pictures on screen.
Hard copy	a print out onto paper of your word processed document. Hard copy gives you some security if your word processor fails.
Hard disk	a storage disk found inside the System Unit. It is capable of holding far more information than a floppy disk.
Hard page break	commanding the word processor to end a page at a particular point in a document.
Hardware	the electronic and mechanical components of a computer system.

Header a line, or a number of lines, which are added automatically at the top of every page of a document you print out. You set the number of lines between the header and the top of the page.

Icon an on-screen picture of a command (see GUI).

Insert adding characters into a document while not erasing existing text by overtyping.

Justification the way in which a line of text appears on screen and on paper. With left justification text begins at the left margin and usually ends short of the right. With full justification text begins at the left margin and ends at the right. With right justification text begins at the right margin and usually ends short of the left margin.

Macro a single keystroke that is programmed to perform a series of keystrokes. Macros are useful when you need to do repetitive tasks.

Menu a list of command options.

Merge inserting information from one document into a certain point in another.

Orphan the first line of a paragraph appearing at the end of a page.

Overtyping a way of typing over text that you have already keyed in without having to erase it.

Page break the end of a page, which can either be hard (inserted by you) or soft (inserted automatically by the computer).

Pagination where the page breaks are in a document.

Paper feed a method by which paper is fed into a printer.

Paragraph indent using the tab facility to start the first line of a paragraph a short distance away from the left-hand margin.

Pitch the horizontal spacing of characters, usually expressed as the number of characters that appear per inch. Knowing the pitch of characters is not so important when word processing, but in desktop publishing work it is important to know exactly where text is on the page.

Proof read checking over a document for errors.

Proportional spacing printing where characters vary in their width, depending on the amount of horizontal space they take up.

Record a set of variable items (fields) such as the name, address and telephone number of a client.

Reformat changing text to take account of changes to it, such as the deletion of characters. This is usually done automatically by the computer.

Ruler line is like a standard ruler. Found at the top or bottom of the screen it shows your position in the document, and also tab settings and margins.

Scrolling movement of the cursor usually vertically, but sometimes horizontally, through a document.

Soft page break a page break that is automatically inserted by the word processor at a pre-set position.

Software the program of instructions that allows computer equipment to perform particular tasks.

Status line a line of information at the top or bottom of the monitor screen that provides information on the position of the cursor and/or the directory and name of the current document.

String a set of characters (a group of letters, digits or punctuation marks) in a document.

System Unit the main box of the computer which contains all the mechanics (such as disk drives) and the electronics of the computer.

Text file the same as an ASCII file.

Tractor feed a device on a printer that allows continuous stationery to be fed through it.

VDU: a Visual Display Unit, or monitor.

Virus a rogue program that upsets the operation of your computer. Viruses can enter your computer through borrowed floppy disks or any disk that has not been checked for a virus. You can buy anti-virus software that will check the condition of a floppy for you.

Undelete recalling deleted text back into a document. This can only be done if your word processor has an undelete command.

Underline a word processor function that puts a line under characters as you type them.

Undo a command that lets you stop half way through a word processing operation without affecting the text.

Widow the last line of a paragraph that appears alone at the top of a page.

Window a section of the monitor screen when it has been split. You can have different documents in each window.

Windows a proprietary brand of software that sits on top of the DOS system and creates a more user-friendly environment which allows you to issue commands by pointing at icons.

Wordwrap a facility on a word processor that automatically takes the cursor down to the next line when the end of the previous line has been reached.

Wraparound the same as wordwrap.

Write protect protecting the information you have stored on a disk from accidental erasure.

WYSIWYG 'What You See Is What You Get'. This means that what you see on the screen is exactly what comes out of the printer.

Appendix

There are many, many word processing packages to choose from. Some of them are very well known, while others are more obscure. Before committing yourself to one package, try to use as many as possible, until you find one that suits your needs and temperament. As a test of user friendliness, immediately attempt to use the word processor with only the minimum of help from the manual. If you find that without too much difficulty you can work most of the major commands then the chances are that this package is reasonably user friendly. If you have to consult the manual frequently on how to do something, then it is probably rather user-unfriendly. Since there is no point in making things difficult for yourself, pick the word processor that does what you want it to in the easiest possible way. A selection of packages is outlined below to give you an idea of what is on the market. All costs are approximate.

Accent for Windows

A Windows-based word processor that supports 32 European languages. It has 17 spellcheckers containing over 3 million words. It is compatible with Word, WordPerfect and other major word processing packages. For the advanced user. Cost £300.

Ami Pro 3.1

Another Windows-based word processor that has a very good range of tools and commands. This is a favourite with many people; it is powerful and easy to use. For the advanced user. Cost £100.

Better Working Word

A value for money word processor with a pretty good range of features. For the intermediate user. Cost £50.

Cicero 2.0

Good range of features. For the intermediate user. Cost £200.

Format PC

This is fine for processing simple documents and, for those with an interest in languages, it can support Russian and Arabic. For the intermediate user. Cost £200.

LetterPerfect 1.0

A reduced version of WordPerfect and without many of its more advanced features. For the beginner. Cost £35.

LEX Elite

Wide range of features, including a calculator for ledgers and cost analysis. For the advanced user. Cost £400.

Lococript Professional 2.0 Plus

Originally written for the Amstrad PCW this word processor features drop down menus and an integrated database so you can combine information. For the beginner. Cost £100.

Lotus Write 2.0

A Windows-based word processor that is a reduced version of Ami Pro and so without its advanced features. For the beginner. Cost £100.

Multiword Prestige

Many good features with an ability to draw lines for forms and diagrams. For the advanced user. Cost £500.

Prisma Office for Windows

A Windows-based word processor with a large spellchecker and thesaurus. For the advanced user. Cost £250.

Professional Write 2.2

A reasonable word processor for the intermediate user. Cost £165.

Protext 6.0

A word processor with a fair number of features for the intermediate user. Cost £175.

Q&A Write 3.0

A word processor with a good number of features. For the advanced user. Cost £60.

Topcopy Professional 2.23

A word processor with a good number of features. It allows multiple columns to be created, a feature not always found on more expensive software. For the intermediate user. Cost £100.

Universal Word for Windows

A multi-lingual package that can support 50 different languages but is still capable of being used by the beginner. Cost £400.

Wiziword 3.0

This is a full WYSIWYG word processor that has the capability to handle scientific equations. For the advanced user. Cost £450.

Word 6.0

A high powered word processor with many features, but one for the advanced user. Cost £285.

Word for Windows 6.0

This is one of the market leaders. Very good range of features, but for the more advanced user. Cost £400.

Wordcraft 6

Especially designed for secretaries who process large amounts of text; very fast, but not that easy to learn. Possesses powerful database for mailshots. For the intermediate to advanced user. Cost £475.

WordPerfect 6.0

The most popular word processor in the world. The latest version includes a spreadsheet and a grammar checker, but commands using quite complicated key sequences so more for the advanced user. A Windows-based version is available for easier usage. Cost £330.

Wordstar 7.0

This is one of the oldest word processors around, but new versions mean that it has many features. A Windows-based version is available. For the advanced user. Cost £400.

Write On

A simple word processor that is good for children, because it can be altered as they become more skilful. Obviously for the beginner. Cost £40.

Further Reading

CHOOSING EQUIPMENT

I Hate Buying a Computer, Jim Felici (Que).
Buy a PC, Mike James (I/O Press).
Beginners Guide to the PC, McKelland and Waixel (Kuma Books).
Technology Tools for Your Home Office, Peter Chatterton (Kogan Page).
Profiting from Your Printer, Frank Booty (Computer Weekly Publications).

COMPUTER MAGAZINES

Computer Shopper
Computer Buyer
PC Direct
PC Magazine
PC Plus
PC Home
Practical PC
PC Review

KEYBOARD SKILLS AND WORD PROCESSING

Advanced Typewriting Skills, Joyce Stananough (McGraw-Hill).
RSA Typewriting Skills Book, (RSA Examination Board).
Keyboarding and Document Production, Alan Whitcomb and Barbara Bowe (Stanley Thomas).
Writing On Disk, Jane Dormer (John Taylor Book Ventures).
Word Processing Secrets for Writers, Michael Banks and Ansell Dibell (Writers Digest Books).
Running Your Own Word Processing Service, Doreen Hulley (Kogan Page).

Numerous manuals and books are available on specific word processing packages.

Index

How to Manage Computers at Work
Graham Jones

Here is a practical step-by-step guide which puts the business needs of the user first. It discusses why a computer may be needed, how to choose the right one and instal it properly; how to process letters and documents, manage accounts, and handle customer and other records and mailing lists. It also explains how to use computers for business presentations, and desktop publishing. If you feel you should be using a computer at work, but are not sure how to start, then this is definitely the book for you. . . and you won't need an electronics degree to start! 'Bags of information in a lingo we can all understand. I strongly recommend the book.' *Progress/NEBS Management Association.* Graham Jones has long experience of handling personal computers for small business management. The Managing Director of a desktop publishing company, he is also author of *How to Start a Business From Home* and *How to Publish a Newsletter* in this Series.

160pp, 1 85703 078 8.

How to Start a Business From Home
Graham Jones

Most people have dreamed of starting their own business from home at some time or other, but how do you begin? The third edition of this popular book contains a wealth of ideas, projects, tips, facts, checklists and quick-reference information for everyone — whether in-between jobs, taking early retirement, or students and others with time to invest. Packed with information on everything from choosing a good business idea and starting up to advertising, book-keeping and dealing with professionals, this book is basic reading for every budding entrepreneur. 'Full of ideas and advice.' *The Daily Mirror.* 'This book is essential — full of practical advice.' *Home Run.* Graham Jones BSc(Hons) is an editor, journalist and lecturer specialising in practical business subjects. His other books include *Fit to Manage* and *The Business of Freelancing.*

176pp illus. 1 85703 126 1. Third edition.

How to Write Business Letters
Ann Dobson

Without proper help, lots of people find it quite hard to cope with even basic business correspondence. Intended for absolute beginners, this book uses fictional characters in a typical business setting to contrast the right and wrong ways to go about things. Taking nothing for granted, the book shows how to plan a letter, how to write and present it, how to deal with requests, how to write and answer complaints, standard letters, personal letters, job applications, letters overseas, and a variety of routine and tricky letters. Good, bad and middling examples are used, to help beginners see for themselves the right and wrong ways of doing things. Ann Dobson is principal of a secretarial training school with long experience of helping people improve their business skills.

160pp illus. 1 85703 104 0.

How to Write A Report
John Bowden

Communicating effectively on paper is an essential skill for todays' business or professional person. Written by an experienced manager and staff trainer, this well-presented handbook provides a very clear step-by-step framework for every individual, whether dealing with professional colleagues, customers, clients, suppliers or junior or senior staff. Contents: Preparation and planning. Collecting and handling information. Writing the report: principles and techniques. Improving your thinking. Improving presentation. Achieving a good writing style. Making effective use of English. How to choose and use illustrations. Choosing paper, covers and binding. Appendices (examples, techniques, checklists), glossary, index. 'Most of us have a need to write a report of some kind at various times, and this book has real value. . . Thoroughly commendable.' *IPS Journal.* John Bowden BSc(Econ) MSc has long experience both as a professional manager in industry, and as a Senior Lecturer running courses in accountancy, auditing and effective communication.

160pp illus. 1 85703 124 5. Second edition.

How to Master Business English
Michael Bennie

Are you communicating effectively? Do your business documents achieve the results you want? Or are they too often ignored or misunderstood? Good communication is the key to success in any business. Whether you are trying to sell a product, answer a query or complaint, or persuade colleagues, the way you express yourself is often as important as what you say. With lots of examples, checklists and questionnaires to help you, the new edition of this book will speed you on your way. 'An excellent book — not in the least dull. . . Altogether most useful for anyone seeking to improve their communication skills.' *IPS Journal*. 'Gives guidance on writing styles for every situation. . . steers the reader through the principles and techniques of effective letter-writing and document-planning.' *First Voice*. 'Useful chapters on grammar, punctuation and spelling. Frequent questionnaires and checklists enable the reader to check progress.' *Focus (Society of Business Teachers)*. 'The language and style is easy to follow. . . Excellent value for money.' *Spoken English*.

208pp illus. 1 85703 129 6. Second edition.

How to Master Book-Keeping
Peter Marshall

Illustrated at every stage with specimen entries, the book will be an ideal companion for students taking LCCI, RSA, BTEC, accountancy technician and similar courses at schools, colleges or training centres. Typical business transactions are used to illustrate all the essential theory, practice and skills required to be effective in a real business setting. 'Has a number of welcome and unusual features. . . The content is broken down into mind-sized chunks and the treatment is generally friendly.' *School Librarian Journal*. 'An interesting approach.' *Association of Business Executive Journal*. 'A complete step-by-step guide. . . each section of the book teaches a useful skill in its own right.' *OwnBase*. 'In addition to providing a useful approach to the teaching and learning of book-keeping skills, the way in which the text is presented should ensure that the book also provides a valuable reference source for revision and prompting.' *Teeline*.

176pp illus. 1 85703 065 6. Second edition.

How to Publish a Newsletter
Graham Jones

Are you planning a community newsletter, business bulletin, house magazine, school newspaper or similar publication? With so many design and print facilities around today there has probably never been a better time to start. Now in an updated new edition, this book guides you through the whole process. 'Good practical stuff . . . Will certainly give you a good enough understanding of the basics to cope with the normal demands of newsletter publishing.' *Writers News*. 'Until now there has been no adequate British guide. . . but that has been remedied in a new book by Graham Jones, *How to Publish a Newsletter*. . . a comprehensive guide to all aspects including the initial concept, design, writing, marketing, finance, contributors, advertising, editing, printing etc.' *Freelance Writing & Photography*. 'Here is a man who knows his subject intimately' *Writers Monthly*. 'Should be of interest to small voluntary groups.' *NCVO News*. Graham Jones is Managing Director of ASPECT, a company which produces house magazines and other publications for client organisations.

176pp illus. 1 85703 166 0. Second edition.

How to do Your Own Advertising
Michael Bennie

'Entrepreneurs and small businesses are flooding the market with new products and services; the only way to beat the competition is successful selling — and that means advertising.' But what can you afford? This book is for anyone who needs — or wants — to advertise effectively, but does not want to pay agency rates. Michael Bennie is Director of Studies at the Copywriting School. 'An absolute must for everyone running their own small business. . . Essential reading. . . Here at last is a practical accessible handbook which will make sure your product or service gets the publicity it deserves.' *Great Ideas Newsletter (Business Innovations Research)*. 'Explains how to put together a simple yet successful advertisement or brochure with the minimum of outside help. . . amply filled with examples and case studies.' *First Voice (National Federation of Self Employed and Small Businesses)*.

176pp illus. 0 7463 0579 6.